The ABBA Guide to Stockholm

Sara Russell

THE... ABBA GUIDE TO STOCKHOLM

PREMIUM PUBLISHING
Stockholm

Premium Publishing
Box 30184
SE-104 25 Stockholm
Sweden

Phone: +46 8 545 689 20
E-Mail: info@premiumpublishing.com
Web: www.premiumpublishing.com

Publisher: Wille Wendt
Project leader: Liska Cersowsky
Project assistant: Roger Holegård
Map graphics: Myran Grafiska

Graphic design & illustrations by Billy Adolfsson: www.billyadolfsson.com

Printed by Fälth & Hässler, Sweden
Paper: MultiArt Silk 130gr

ISBN: 978-91-89136-54-0
The book is also available in a German language version. ISBN: 978-91-89136-69-4

Back in 1974, ABBA put Sweden on the world map by winning the Eurovision Song Contest. The band became the most well-known Swedish pop export and gained immense global success – which still continues to this day! Largely due to ABBA's achievements, Sweden has strengthened its position as one of the world's leading music producing countries, with its capital at the heart of the action.

Stockholm is not only the home of acts like Roxette, Europe and Robyn but has also established itself as a creative centre for numerous international pop stars such as Britney Spears, Celine Dion, Backstreet Boys and Jennifer Lopez who have had many of their hits written, produced and recorded here!

Stockholm is of course the home town of ABBA, and it was from here their successful careers were master-minded by Stikkan "Stig" Anderson. Every year more than one million international visitors come to Stockholm to experience its wide range of cultural offerings, pulsating night life, modern Scandinavian architecture and, last but not least, its famous traditional meatballs!

With *The ABBA Guide to Stockholm*, you can now at last walk in the footsteps of Sweden's biggest ever pop band. Experience the city's many entertainment attractions, museums, concert halls, restaurants, cafés, shops and of course the beautiful and unique archipelago with its zillions of islands.

While I am sure your discovery of ABBA's Stockholm will be enjoyable and exciting, it is important to note that any private addresses featured in this book have absolutely no current connection to ABBA or its members. They are included purely as reference for location purposes. Please respect the privacy of the people who now live at those addresses.

Have fun and enjoy your ABBA-flavoured stay in Stockholm!

Sam

Lois

Anni-Frid Lyngstad ("Frida") was born on 15th November 1945 in Ballangen outside of Narvik in Norway. Known as "the dark one", Frida has been heavily involved in environmental issues in the years since ABBA, as well as campaigning against drug use. Best ABBA solos: *Knowing Me, Knowing You, Fernando* and *Super Trouper.* Frida lives in Zermatt, Switzerland and Skåne, Sweden.

Björn Ulvaeus was born on 25th April 1945 in Gothenburg. He's the one "without the beard" even though he has actually had one since 1981. Björn wrote the lyrics to the majority of ABBA songs (several early ones were written by manager Stig Anderson). He has been the most involved ABBA member behind *Mamma Mia!* the stage show since its inception. Best ABBA solos: *Does Your Mother Know* and *Man In The Middle.* Björn lives in Djursholm, north of Stockholm.

Benny Andersson was born on 16th December 1946 in Stockholm. Known as "the one with the beard", Benny has music running through his blood and is the only ABBA member you could still see performing live – with BAO! (Benny Andersson's Orchestra). He wrote most of the ABBA music; *Chess* and all of the music for *Kristina från Duvemåla.* He re-recorded and arranged the music for *Mamma Mia! The Movie.* Best ABBA solos: *Suzy Hang-Around* and *Intermezzo No.1* (instrumental). Benny lives in central Stockholm.

Agnetha Fältskog was born on 5th April 1950 in Jönköping. Known as "the blonde one" during the ABBA years and beyond, she is still being portrayed by the press as a recluse. In reality she simply doesn't enjoy being in the limelight and prefers to spend time at home with her family. Best ABBA solos: *The Winner Takes It All, SOS* and *The Day Before You Came.* Agnetha lives at Ekerö, west of Stockholm.

...Contents

Östermalm/Gärdet

Djurgården

Outside Central Stockholm

1

Sheraton Hotel

Tegelbacken 6

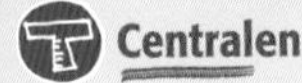
Centralen

3, 53, 62, 65

www.sheratonstockholm.com

Now part of the Starwood hotel chain, the Sheraton is a 5-star hotel in a prime location overlooking Gamla Stan and Lake Mälaren with great views of Stadshuset. It was voted Best Business Hotel of 2006 and has 465 guest rooms, two restaurants and two bars.

The hotel room scene featured in *ABBA – The Movie* was actually filmed at the Sheraton in Stockholm, not in Perth, Australia as implied in the film. This is the scene where ABBA review the newspapers and the headline *Agnetha's Bottom Tops Show* is read out. You will notice that a carefully placed thumb actually hides the word "*Dull*" before "*Show*" which makes the true headline very disappointing. Agnetha remains upbeat in the scene by exclaiming, *"At least I did something for the show!"*

Filmed in June 1977, Agnetha was mid-way through her pregnancy so camera angles were carefully worked out so that you didn't see much more than just her head and shoulders.

In a break from filming, some pictures were taken on a top floor hotel room balcony with a magnificent view of Stadshuset (see p. 40) in the background. Agnetha and Björn were photographed in the dressing gowns they were wearing in the film. Agnetha was also pictured wearing just a towel!

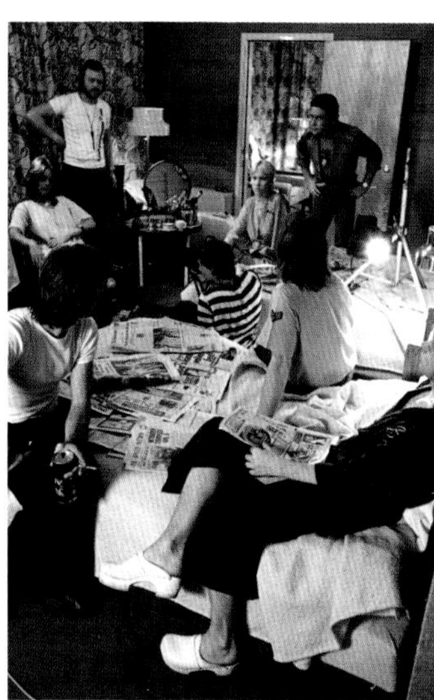

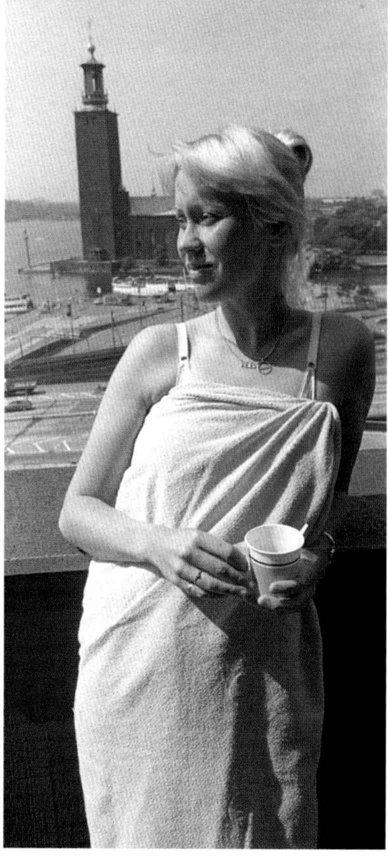

2

Kungliga Operan

Royal Opera House
Gustav Adolfs Torg

 Kungsträdgården  2, 43, 55, 62, 65

www.operan.se

Kungliga Operan that exists today was built in 1899. It has a magnificent golden foyer and elegant marbled staircase which leads to an auditorium seating about 1,200 people. Guided tours are available weekdays during the summer months. At the rear of Kungliga Operan is Café Opera and Operakällaren (see p. 13).

Wearing wonderful old-fashioned costumes, ABBA performed *Dancing Queen* at a special Gala on the eve of the wedding of King Carl Gustav to Silvia Sommerlath on 18th June 1976 at Kungliga Operan. The Gala was shown live on Swedish TV, called *Det låg ett skimmer över Gustafs dagar* (There was a shimmer during the Gustavian days) which is a quote from a famous poem by the Swedish poet Esaias Tegnér. It was assumed that the song had been especially written for the future Queen Silvia but this was not the case as it had been written the previous year and performed earlier in the year in both Germany and Australia.

In 1993 Frida helped to organise a variety concert to mark the 50th birthday of Queen Silvia. The show was broadcast live on 22nd December 1993 from Kungliga Operan, called *Ja må hon leva* (Yes may she live). In act one, Frida appeared on stage as one of three fairies, dressed in a fetching orange outfit to narrate the Queen's story and then later appeared on stage as herself to sing a fantastic a capella version of *Dancing Queen* with The Real Group. It was released on The Real Group's 1994 album *Varför får man inte bara vara som man är?* (Why can't I be the way I am?).

In 1997, Benny was appointed to the Board of the Royal Swedish Opera by the Swedish Government.

3

Opera Källaren

The Opera Cellar
Karl XIIs torg

www.operakallaren.se

 **Kungsträdgården**  **2, 43, 55, 62, 65**

With an entrance at the rear of Kungliga Operan, Operakällaren first opened in 1787. It was firstly transformed into a modern restaurant in the 1860s. Today Operakällaren is an exclusive and very popular bar/restaurant complex in the pulsating city centre.

Parts of the 1985 TV programme *A For Agnetha* were filmed in front of Opera-källaren. The opening scene shows Agnetha feeding the birds by the freezing water's edge and you can see the corner of Operakällaren in the background. If the area looks familiar, it's because Björn made a series of brief promotional films for Australian ABC's *Countdown* programme in early 1976. In one of them, he is just along the water's edge from where Agnetha stood feeding the birds around nine years later.

Five super-Swedes: ABBA and Ingemar Stenmark at the Expressen spring party in 1977.

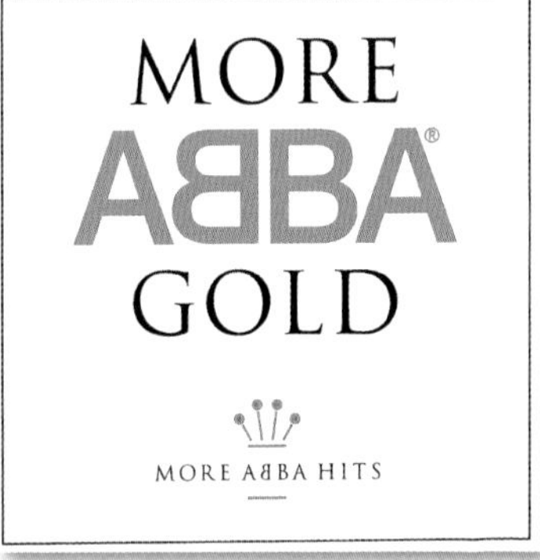

On 18th April 1977, all four members of ABBA participated in the annual spring party at Operakällaren, an award ceremony organised by the Swedish newspaper Expressen during the 70s. Several well-known Swedes were there including champion slalom skier Ingemar Stenmark and Forbes, the group representing Sweden in the 1977 Eurovision Song Contest. ABBA was awarded the Golden Wasp by the newspaper Expressen for the TV special *ABBA-dabba-dooo!!* which had been voted by the readers as the best TV show of 1976.

In October 1993, Björn, Frida and Benny reunited at Operakällaren at a reception hosted by PolyGram where they were presented with awards for album sales of both *ABBA Gold* and *More ABBA Gold*. They were photographed with a 5-CD award which represented sales of 5 million copies worldwide for *ABBA Gold*.

4

Sankt Jacobs Kyrka

Saint Jacob's Church
Västra Trädgårdsgatan

 **Kungsträdgården**  **2, 43, 47, 62, 65, 69**

Sankt Jacobs kyrka, just off Kungsträdgården, is dedicated to apostle Saint James the Greater. It opened in 1643 and offers services in both Swedish and English.

Stig Anderson's funeral service took place at Sankt Jacobs on Friday 10th October 1997. It was attended by Frida, Benny and Björn. Agnetha was unwell and sent a wreath saying "Thank you and farewell". The funeral was broadcast live by Swedish TV. Stig is buried at Galärvarvskyrkogården on Djurgården (see p. 82).

After the service, Björn, Benny and their wives were photographed walking away from the church through Kungsträdgården.

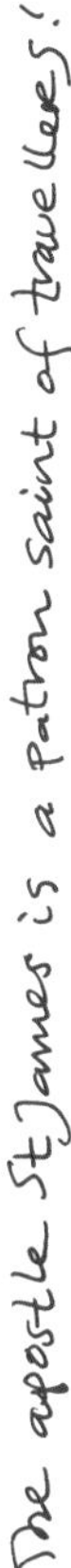

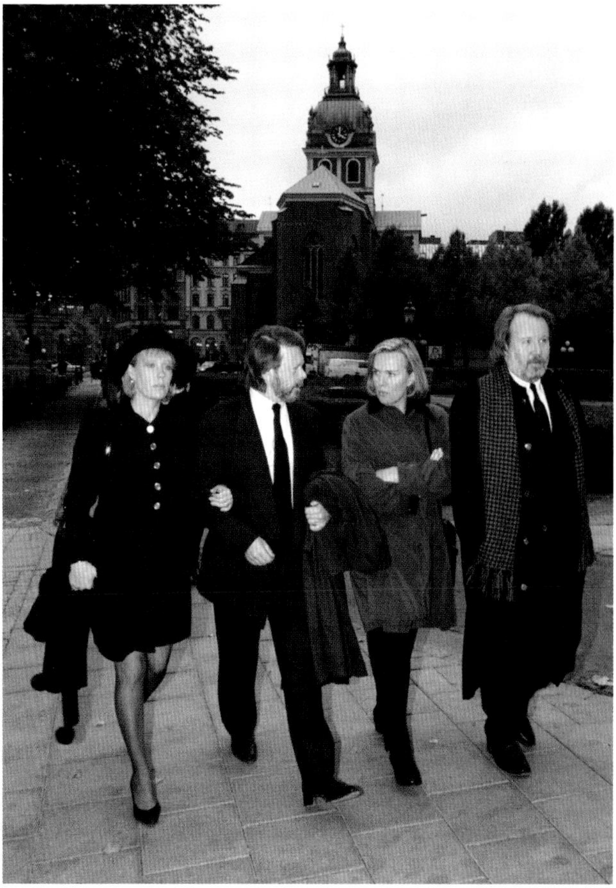

5

Hamburger Börs

Jakobsgatan 6

 **Kungsträdgården**  **2, 43, 62, 65, 69**

www.hamburgerbors.se

Situated just behind Sankt Jacobs kyrka (see p. 15), Hamburger Börs has been a popular meeting place in the centre of Stockholm for more than 250 years. The original building was torn down in 1970 and then rebuilt. It's a very lively place to see revues and floorshows with a meal – but don't expect to see hamburgers on the menu!

On 1st February 1969, Benny's group The Hep Stars opened their new show at Hamburger Börs and it was that night that Frida met Benny properly, after a very brief initial meeting in Malmö. Six months later, they got engaged at Hamburger Börs on 18th August 1969 at the opening night of Frida's latest cabaret show.

6

China Teatern

The China Theatre
Berzelii Park

www.berns.se

 Kungsträdgården  47, 62, 69, 76

China Teatern is a private theatre in Stockholm located at Berzelii Park at Nybroplan, very close to Dramaten (The Royal Dramatic Theatre). Originally built in 1929 as a cinema, it has also been used as a theatre for musicals, comedies and revues.

It was here on 26th December 1977 that the Swedish première of *ABBA – The Movie* took place. All four ABBA members attended. It was just three weeks after Agnetha gave birth to her and Björn's son Christian.

The theatre scenes in the music video for *The Day Before You Came* were filmed on the stage and auditorium of China Teatern. Whilst present for the filming of the music video, photographer Anders Hanser took some group photos in front of a mural on the stairs leading up from the theatre foyer.

In 1996, Frida made the TV special *Mitt i livet* (In the middle of life) to complement her newly released album *Djupa andetag* (Deep breaths). As part of the documentary, the song *Sista valsen med dig* (Last dance with you) was filmed at the China Theatre with Frida perched on the edge of the stage.

7

Nordiska Kompaniet

Hamngatan 18

www.nk.se

 Kungsträdgården  47, 62, 69, 76

NK – short for Nordiska Kompaniet – is known as "the great department store". Founded by Josef Sachs in 1902, the store offers best quality goods from all around the world, has five floors and over 100 separate departments. The Swedish Royal Family is known to shop here. The illuminated circular NK sign is a distinctive sight on the night-time Stockholm skyline.

In 1982 the street scenes for the music video *Head Over Heels* were filmed in and outside NK. Frida and Björn, who played a married couple, were seen in the store with Frida trying on hats while Björn looks on yawning. Then, as Frida bustles along the street, Björn lags behind laden down with her shopping bags. This was all filmed in Hamngatan just outside NK, with the Nordea Bank next door.

As part of the promotional *A For Agnetha* programme in 1985, Agnetha was filmed singing *Just One Heart.* Where you see her walking towards the camera, she is on her way from Hamngatan to Norrmalmstorg, just along from NK and opposite the old Polar offices at Hamngatan 11 (see p. 20).

8

Polar Music Offices

Hamngatan 11 / Norrmalmstorg

 **Kungsträdgården**  **47, 62, 69, 76**

On 9th November 1981, Polar Music moved out of the building at Baldersgatan 1 (see p. 32) and into new offices in central Stockholm at Hamngatan 11 – so for the final year of ABBA they were based out of this office.

On 16th January 1986, ABBA reformed to perform *Tivedshambo* as a surprise for Stig Anderson's appearance on the Swedish TV show *Här är ditt liv* (This is your life). The song was one of Stig's first ever compositions. Görel Hanser was standing next to the camera holding up the lyrics for them while they sang in Benny's attic studio.

Before this performance, Frida and Agnetha hadn't met for two years. This was the very last performance by the ABBA members together that was seen by the public. The Polar Music offices had its headquarters at Hamngatan 11 for more than ten years, all through the solo and *Chess* years. British Airways had residency at the offices for many years after that. Today the offices are inhabited by other companies.

YAMAHA

9

Södra Blasieholmshamnen 8

www.grandhotel.se

Grand Hôtel is a classy five star hotel in the very heart of Stockholm which opened in 1874. It commands fantastic views over the harbour, Gamla Stan and Kungliga Slottet. Grand Hôtel hosts the annual Polar Music Prize banquet after the actual ceremony.

In 1976, Frida and Benny were interviewed outside Grand Hôtel for the Australian ABC programme *Countdown*. During the interview they were interrupted by the regular war alert exercise, happening on the first Monday in March, June, September and December at 3pm. You can hear the sirens in the background of the video, sounding all across the city.

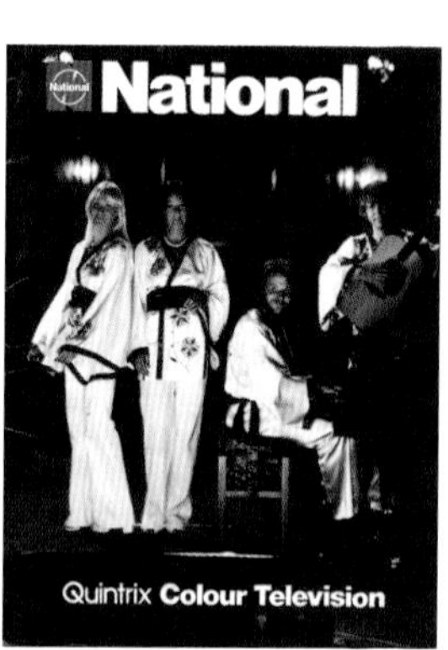

In summer 1976 ABBA filmed five TV commercials for the Japanese electronics firm National (now Panasonic). One of the five commercials was filmed entirely in the Ballroom of Grand Hôtel with the girls wearing the well-known cat costumes, for the first and only time with white trousers. Another snippet of the commercials showed them wearing the kimono costumes introduced earlier that year. The adverts were broadcast exclusively in Australia as a means of financing part of their 1977 Australian concert tour.

For the commercials ABBA had recorded new lyrics – written by the advertising company – to the tune of *Fernando*, stating how wonderful National was.

Other parts of the National adverts were filmed at Drottningholm (see p. 122) and in Frida and Benny's flat in Gamla Stan (see p. 56).

Frida co-presented a series of four variety shows in summer 1981 at Grand Hôtel called *Lite grand i örat* (A little something for the ear). Her co-host was Claes af Geijerstam who toured with ABBA as their sound engineer. Claes and Frida started each show with the song *Let's Get This Show On The Road.*

Many of the ABBA gang were involved in the shows – choreographer Graham Tainton, musical director Anders Eljas and musicians Lasse Wellander, Rutger Gunnarsson, Per Lindvall and Åke Sundqvist amongst others. The shows were a mixture of comedy and music with a few novelty variety acts thrown in for good measure.

In the 1985 programme *A For Agnetha,* ABBA's blonde singer can be seen walking along the water's edge past some boats – in fact she is walking towards Grand Hôtel when someone bumps into her, recognises her and says, *"But aren't you..?"*

Some of the Lois Jeans and t-shirt promotion photos were taken in front of Grand Hôtel. ABBA stood facing the hotel with their backs to the water and some of the shots show Kungliga Slottet (see p. 48) in the background. They also posed in front of Stadshuset (see p. 40).

On the morning of the Swedish première of *Mamma Mia! The Movie* on 4th July 2008, there was a press conference at Grand Hôtel with most of the leading actors. Benny and Björn stood alongside the cast and creative team for the press call, armed with pre-sales awards of the cast soundtrack for the film.

.... did you know that Meryl, at the age of (12) studied to be an opera singer !!

Konsert Huset

The Concert Hall
Hötorget 8

www.konserthuset.se

Built between 1923 and 1926, Konserthuset is the home of the Swedish Royal Philharmonic Orchestra and a major concert venue. It is also is the venue for the Nobel Prize ceremony and, in recent years, the Polar Music Prize.

The Polar Music Prize was inaugurated by Stig Anderson in 1989 through a donation to the Royal Swedish Academy of Music. The prize is awarded to a musician or musicians of any nationality for "*significant achievements in music and/or musical life, or for achievements which are believed to be of great potential importance for the advancement of music and/or musical life*". Past winners include Sir Paul McCartney (1992), Sir Elton John (1995), Ray Charles (1998), Stevie Wonder (1999) and Burt Bacharach (2001).

On 11th January 1975, ABBA performed live at Konserthuset as part of their tour of Nordic countries. It was a more elaborate concert than they had staged before and included special effects. This tour was intended to compensate to the fans in some way for their cancelled performances the previous summer in the aftermath of their Eurovision win.

Note: At the back of the building, Frida was filmed crossing the junction of Kungsgatan/Sveavägen for the music video *Head Over Heels* in 1982. The steps where Frida is seen running up and down is one block away from Konserthuset where Kungsgatan meets Malmskillnadsgatan; and the doorway where she slips over is almost directly oppposite the steps at Kungsgatan 35.

Alexandra's Disco

Döbelnsgatan 3

Hötorget

56, 59

Alexandra's disco was a very popular nightclub in Stockholm in the 1970s and 1980s, owned by Alexandra Charles, friend of ABBA and queen of the 70s and 80s nightclub scene. The club moved a number of times in its existence. Firstly located on Biblioteksgatan 5, it moved to Döbelnsgatan 3 in 1977. It moved one last time to Birger Jarlsgatan in 1984, before closing permanently four years later.

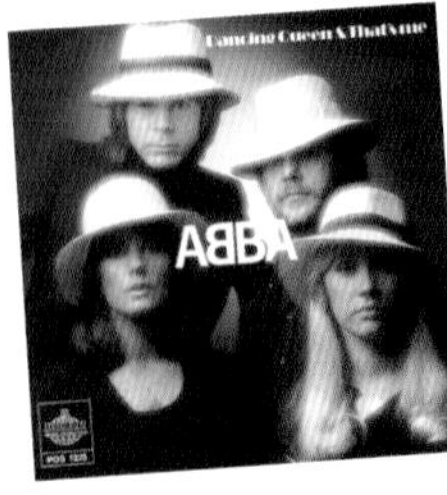

On 2nd February 1976, the music video for ABBA's most successful single, *Dancing Queen* was filmed at Döbelnsgatan 3. Who could ever forget the sight of the two girls, full of energy, dancing on the stage and smiling as they sang in front of a small audience of, what turned out to be, children? *Dancing Queen* was ABBA's only US No. 1 single and hit the top spot in many other countries.

At that time, the location belonged to the discotheque Fattighuset, which got its name from the almshouse that was situated here in the 17th century. Alexandra's disco moved to this address just a year later.

It was here, when Alexandra's disco was located at Döbelnsgatan 3, that the photo session for the cover of ABBA's 1979 album, *Voulez-Vous* took place. The photographer was Ola Lager who also took the cover photographs for the albums *Waterloo, ABBA* and *Arrival*. He had wanted to do something new with mirrors and knew Alexandra's disco had mirrored walls so the photo-shoot was arranged there. He had wanted two pictures of each member (one picture, one a reflection) but the session didn't turn out as expected. Instead, there is a hint of a rear reflection of Benny in the background between Frida and Agnetha. The classy, sophisticated look complemented the direction the music was taking. Benny was holding a neon light to create "something different" to look at.

Another shot from this session was used for the single release of *Does Your Mother Know* in several countries including Australia, Ecuador, France, Germany, India, Italy, Mexico, USA and Yugoslavia. The Netherlands and Portugal used the same picture but chose to reverse it. The UK and France were also blessed with 12" picture disc versions of the album.

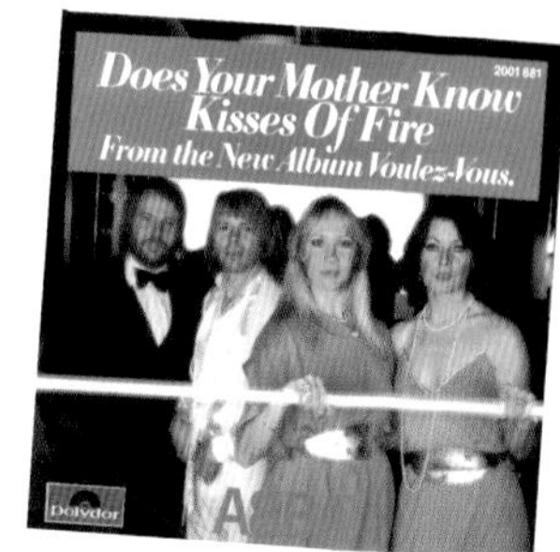

In 1999 when asked to recall memories of ABBA for the opening of an ABBA exhibition at Nordiska Museet (The Nordic Museum), club owner Alexandra Charles remembered, *"My greatest memory is from Döbelnsgatan. Benny and Micke Tretow came straight from the Polar Studio with a new recording. 'Play it here', they said. It was after closing. So we put it on. A record that nobody else had heard. It was an amazing feeling."*

Metronome Studios

Now Atlantis Studio
Karlbergsvägen 57

 S:t Eriksplan  42, 47

www.atlantisgramm.se

The studios started life as a small cinema in 1941 until it was closed in 1959 and transformed into Metronome Recording Studio. Brothers Anders and Lasse Burman and their friend Börje Ekberg masterminded the studio and record label. The first recording artists were known for their jazz records – people like Charlie Norman, Alice Babs, Quincy Jones and Harry Arnold.

Throughout the 60s, the singers and musicians who passed through Metronome's doors read like a "Who's who" of Swedish music. For many years it was the only major recording studio in Stockholm – meaning every major (and minor) Swedish recording artist laid down tracks at Metronome at some point.

Metronome is just a short distance away from the location of Polar Music Studio (see p. 34) which was built due to Metronome being so busy. The name was changed to Atlantis Studios in 1983.

Björn's band The Hootenanny Singers recorded at Metronome Studios. Agnetha and Frida also did some recordings here during their pre-ABBA solo careers. This is where Björn first met ABBA's sound engineer Michael B Tretow.

ABBA recorded the following albums at Metronome Studio – much of *Ring Ring*, all of *Waterloo*, parts of *ABBA* and, except for the basic backing track of *Dancing Queen*, all of *Arrival*. Benny and Björn also worked there with some other Polar artists, like Ted Gärdestad and Lena Andersson.

Agnetha and Frida were filmed recording the vocals for *Dancing Queen* at Metronome Studio as part of the TV documentary *Mr Trendsetter* about Stig Anderson in 1975. It turned out to be the only time ABBA were filmed while recording in the studio for real!

A TV documentary about Metronome founder Anders Burman was filmed here in 1998 called *Ulvaeus och Gessle i Burmans spår* (Ulvaeus and Gessle in Burman's footsteps). Björn and Per Gessle from Roxette talked with Anders Burman in the middle of the studio around a piano, recalling memories and experiences from their recording days.

In 2004, Agnetha recorded *My Colouring Book* at Atlantis Studio and her music videos for *If I Thought You'd Ever Change Your Mind, When You Walk In The Room* and *Sometimes When I'm Dreaming* were all filmed here.

In 2007, Benny together with original ABBA musicians Lasse Wellander, Rutger Gunnarsson and Per Lindvall re-recorded the music for *Mamma Mia! The Movie* here at Atlantis Studio.

13

Hard Rock Café

Sveavägen 75

 Odenplan/Rådmansgatan  2, 4, 40, 42 www.hardrock.se

After London, the first European Hard Rock Café to open was in Stockholm in April 1985. Like all restaurants in the Hard Rock franchise, the walls are adorned with instruments, albums, awards and memorabilia from world-famous artists and groups.

In the past, no trip to Stockholm would have been complete for an ABBA fan without a visit to the Hard Rock Café situated at the junction of Odengatan and Sveavägen.

If you were lucky, you could get to sit in the "ABBA corner" – a section of the restaurant completely devoted to the Swedish "Fab Four"! On the walls there were photos, discs and memorabilia galore. There also used to be a secret ABBA room upstairs which you could visit under staff supervision, containing dozens of framed awards.

But time passes and things change. Since the restaurant had a refurbishment, the ABBA corner and the ABBA room upstairs are no longer there. Instead, there are just two small wall displays, one containing a fake fur coat owned by Agnetha and signed on the inside lining, a British *Star Monthly* magazine and a copy of *ABBA For The Record* and the other hardly worth mentioning – an award for *ABBA – The Album* and an edition of *Chart Songwords* with ABBA on the cover.

14

Tyrgatan Cover Session

Tyrgatan 8

 Tekniska Högskolan  4

Two blocks away from the Polar Music offices (see p. 32) is Tyrgatan. This is a special road because the cover picture to the *ABBA* album was taken there. The Rolls Royce that ABBA were sitting in was parked in Tyrgatan when Ola Lager took the photograph. This elegant car was once owned by Swedish industrial magnate Ivar Kreuger. The people peering through the car window were just passers-by who were asked if they wouldn't mind looking through the window for a photo-shoot!

Ola Lager's wife worked as a stylist at that time. For this photo-shoot she borrowed a room in an advertising agency on this road, where the group could change clothes. Tyrgatan was – and still is – a quiet street with very little traffic which made it the perfect place to take the photograph.

Today there is a flag pole just above the place where the car was parked.

15

Polar Music Offices

Baldersgatan 1

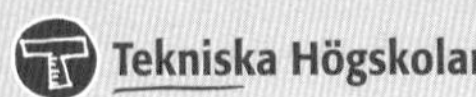 Tekniska Högskolan  4

From summer 1975, ABBA's headquarters was based at modern offices at Baldersgatan 1, in the upmarket area of Östermalm. The corner of the building is quite distinctive with the main entrance being just around the corner of the street through large iron gates.

An image of the corner of the building was included in one of the 1976 Australian bubble gum cards and an artist's impression of the building was used on Stig's Polar Music letterhead – featured in a letter from him in the 1977 tour programme.

POLAR MUSIC H.Q.
No. 22 of 72 B

The top two floors were rented to an insurance company leaving the bottom two floors for Stig Anderson, Görel Johnsen (later to become Hanser) and Polar employee Hans "Berka" Berqkvist.

Benny and Björn had their office on the ground floor next to a room where Agnetha and Frida could practice their dance moves with choreographer Graham Tainton. The walls of this office were adorned with awards and gold discs and the office also contained a TV set, a piano and a large white circular coffee table around which many TV interviews were filmed.

In 1980, a representative of the Dutch ABBA fan club met Björn for the TV show *ABBA, daar vraag je me wat* (ABBA, now you're asking me something) to talk about the new album release of *Super Trouper* which was one of the last times we saw Björn without a beard.

Polar Music moved from Baldersgatan 1 to Hamngatan 11 (see p. 20) in November 1981. For some years afterwards, Baldersgatan 1 was home to the Swedish Police Federation but is now the headquarters for the Swedish Society of Nursing.

16

Polar Music Studios

S:t Eriksgatan 58

 S:t Eriksplan  3, 4, 77

Polar Music Studios opened with a big reception and photo call on 18th May 1978. The building was the Riviera cinema overlooking a stretch of water on Kungsholmen and in a previous life it was even a giant swimming complex. The team of Benny, Björn, sound engineer Michael B Tretow and manager Stig Anderson decided to convert parts of the building into a recording studio after encountering massive problems in finding sufficient studio time in Sweden. They decided to build their own studio rather than go abroad and record. It was bought for 30 million Swedish Kronor and allowed ABBA and other Polar Music artists to consolidate their recording activities in one location. It should be noted that even though ABBA were the owners of the building, they shared it with a number of tenants.

Inside the entrance was a magnificent blue carpet with the Polar Studios logo in white. In the foyer was "the music machine", a huge piece of art by the designer of ABBA's album covers and stage sets, Rune Söderqvist. It was built in 1978, consisting of drums, brass instruments, an old square piano and a chime. It could play *Thank You For The Music.*

Michael B Tretow told the official ABBA Magazine in 1979, *"We bought all the best equipment we could at the time, but the electronics industry is constantly improving its products and new studios are springing up all the time. I have no doubt that our technical specifications have already been eclipsed in some areas."*

From the eight-sided control room with large glass windows, Michael could see, as well as hear, every musician in each of the five separate rooms of "acoustical environments". The inner walls of one of the areas, mainly used for recording drums, was a memorable continuous mural of clouds and blue sky, making it look much bigger than it was with its 251m^2 of floor space. Michael continued, *"We can get over 40 musicians in here at one time, all housed in booths to suit their own instruments. For instance a whole string section can be housed in its own highly 'reflective' area whilst the guitars and vocals stay in the 'non-reflective' zone. The drum booth takes two drummers and with timpani and tuned percussion, and choirs can be completely isolated acoustically. The Polar Studios can supply you with almost everything except hiss, noise, distortion and a decent cup of coffee!"*

The first track completed in the brand new studio was *Summer Night City* but mixing the song wasn't as plain sailing as they'd hoped and over the years Benny, Björn and sound engineer Michael B Tretow have all freely admitted that the track caused them major headaches.

On 5th September 1979, ABBA's music video for *Gimme! Gimme! Gimme! (A Man After Midnight)* was filmed in the studios. The song was already recorded; the performance was purely for the video. At the same time a video for the Spanish version of *I Have A Dream* called *Estoy Soñando* was made.

Numerous interviews for TV programmes were filmed in the studios over the final few ABBA years, most notably Benny's interviews for *20/20* for US TV in 1979, and for the TV show *Freeze Frame* in 1982. Also worth a mention is the documentary *Words & Music* from 1980.

ABBA's best-selling (and final three) albums were all recorded in Studio A at Polar Studios – most of *Voulez-Vous,* all of *Super Trouper* (except for the live recording of *The Way Old Friends Do*) and all of *The Visitors*. Their last album was recorded on the studio's new 3M digital recorder and so became one of

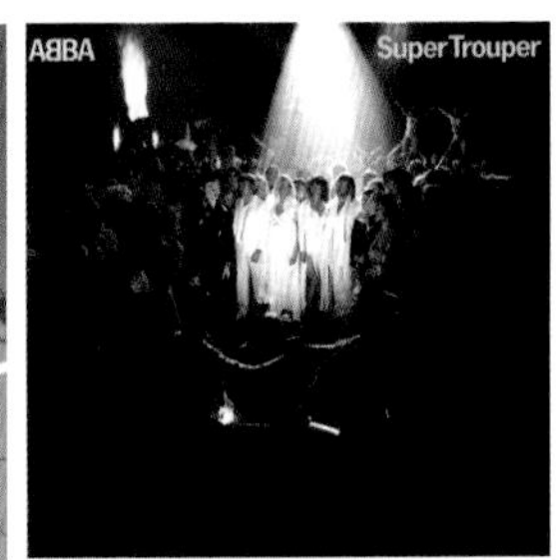

the first digital mainstream pop records. The backing track for *Voulez Vous* was recorded in Miami, the only part of any studio-recorded ABBA track taped outside of Sweden.

In 1982, Frida's album *Something's Going On* was recorded at Polar with producer Phil Collins at the helm. During the recording, the TV documentary *Something's Going On – The Making Of A Record Album* was made, with lots of footage at the studios.

The following year, Agnetha, with the help of producer Mike Chapman, recorded her solo album *Wrap Your Arms Around Me* with UK band Smokie singing the backing vocals. In 1984, she also recorded her album *Eyes Of A Woman* here.

In 1984, Benny and Björn recorded the musical *Chess* in the studio together with Tommy Körberg, Elaine Paige and Barbara Dickson amongst others.

In 1985 and 1987, they also worked on recordings for *Gemini* and Josefin Nilsson (1993) at Polar Studios. Fast forward to 1996 and Frida found herself in the upstairs Studio B with producer Anders Glenmark to record her *Djupa andetag* (Deep breaths) album.

Throughout its existence, Polar Music Studios attracted recording artists from all over the world and included such names as Led Zeppelin, Genesis, Joan Armatrading, The Ramones, Céline Dion, Alice Cooper, Roxette, The Rolling Stones and The Backstreet Boys.

When ABBA stopped recording, the Polar Studio was taken over by Stig Anderson's daughter Marie, her husband & artist Tomas Ledin and Managing Director Lennart Östlund who had been there from the start as a sound engineer, then producer.

At some point they must have sold the property to the existing tenants, who formed a housing cooperative and thus became the joint landlord. This in turn meant that Polar were now forced to pay rent for their space.

The end was all pretty sad. In 2004 the studios closed because the rent had more than doubled in price. Marie Ledin said, *"We have been in long negotiations with the landlord but have not been able to reach an agreement, so we have to shut down the studio."*

Polar attempted to preserve the studio as far back as 1999 and applied for funds from the Cultural Department but were denied due to the unique architectural construction – the studio was built as suspended rooms which hung freely *"like boxes within a box"* and without any walls touching each other. A few rubber blocks were wedged under the floor and between the ceiling and the roof for support. That way, when musicians played their instruments, there was no leakage of soundwaves and each could be heard in isolation.

As Michael B Tretow says in the book *From ABBA to Mamma Mia!* (Anders Hanser and Carl Magnus Palm), *"The cool thing about the Polar studio was that we could record strings at the same time as we recorded the loudest trumpets and trombones ever."* The studio was thus labelled as "furniture" because the walls weren't really the walls and 'furniture' could not be saved by the cultural memorial law.

Benny's response to one journalist who enquired whether it should be turned into a museum was, *"Museum? No, I think Vasa is better. Of course it's sad that the studio disappears, but music history isn't in the walls, it's not in the premises itself. It's possibly inside the people who happened to be there at the time."*

The studio was stripped and some of the parts were sold at an auction. Pieces of furniture including a stool signed by Frida were up for grabs, as well as the mandolin used in the *Fernando* recording (whilst noting that song wasn't actually recorded at Polar Studios!). Some of the blue sky and cloud panels were also up for auction.

Although many of ABBA's most famous songs up to 1978 were recorded elsewhere, Polar Music Studios became to ABBA what Abbey Road Studios was to The Beatles.

Polar Studios closed its door on 1st May 2004 nearly 26 years after it opened. The premises are now a gym.

ALICE COOPER
.... Led Zeppelin, Roxette The Ramones
Rolling stones
Celine Dion

Stadshuset

City Hall
Hantverkargatan 1

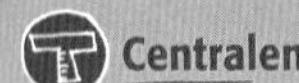

Centralen

3, 62

www.stockholm.se/cityhall

Stadshuset is situated on the edge of lake Mälaren on the island of Kungsholmen and can be seen from most parts of the city. Attracting around 400,000 visitors a year, its massive square tower is 105m high and is topped with the three golden crowns which are the national symbol of Sweden.

The stunning building opened in 1923 and was designed by Sweden's most renowned architect, Ragnar Östberg, who incidentally also designed Stig Anderson's house on Djurgården (see p. 104). It is the venue for the annual Nobel Prize festivities, always on 10th December. On a daily basis it is the home of the Municipal Council for the City of Stockholm. Your efforts to climb the 365 steps of the tower will be rewarded with a truly breathtaking view across Stockholm.

As with most of the main tourist attractions, there is an ABBA connection or two. The earliest was in 1955 when Benny was eight years old. He was playing accordion at a function at Stadshuset and this was where he made his début as a stage performer.

Being the symbol of Stockholm, Stadshuset showed up in the background when, in late summer of 1975, ABBA posed for a photo session wearing Lois Jeans and t-shirts at Evert Taubes Terrass (see p. 60).

When Björn was interviewed by the Australian TV programme *Countdown* in February 1976, he was standing at the water's edge at Söder Mälarstrand on Södermalm affording a lovely winter view of Stadshuset directly from across the water. In the interview Björn pointed to Stadshuset and described it as the place where *"all the politicians gather and talk for days and days!"*

In 1977 during filming of the bedroom scene in *ABBA – The Movie* at the Sheraton Hotel, photos of Agnetha and Björn were taken showing Stadshuset in the background (see p. 10).

In 1987 Agnetha was filmed climbing to the top of the tower at Stadshuset as part of the *A For Agnetha* programme, which promoted her *Eyes Of A Woman* album.

Agnetha's music video for the single *I Wasn't The One (Who Said Goodbye)*, a duet with Peter Cetera (who does not appear in the video), was filmed extensively around Stadshuset and Gamla Stan in 1987.

On 26th September 2008, Benny was bestowed with an Honorary Doctorate from Stockholm University's Faculty of Humanities. The ceremony took place at Stadshuset. In an interview filmed after the ceremony, Benny admitted the highest qualifications he had were a compulsory school certificate and a driving licence!

On 18th June 2009, a stunning looking Agnetha attended the 85th birthday reception for Countess Marianne Bernadotte with her daughter Linda.

18

Katarina Hissen

The Katarina Lift
Slussen

 Slussen  2, 3, 43, 53, 55, 71, 76

Katarinahissen at Slussen was erected in 1883. The lift takes you 38m up to the old, higher-up streets of Mosebacke where there are fantastic views over the waterfront and Gamla Stan.

Benny's group The Hep Stars filmed a scene for their music video *Bald Headed Woman* at the top of Katarinahissen in 1965. It showed Benny on the guitar!

LEAD SINGER Svenne Hedlund is on crutches after breaking his ankle jumping from an amp at a Hep Stars concert!

Hissentré
HISSEN
KATARINAHISSEN
KILLERS
JOAN BAEZ
D'ESPAIRSRAY
ULF
LUNDELL
SOMMAR
2009

Hotel Rival

Mariatorget 3

 Mariatorget  43, 55, 66

www.rival.se

In 2001, together with businessmen Christer Sandahl and Christer Hägglund, Benny invested several million Swedish Kronor into the old Aston Hotel and cinema Rival. They had it renovated into a fantastic modern hotel whilst re-capturing the glamour of the original hotel from the 1930s. They also included a café, bakery, restaurant, bar, bistro and a cinema complex. It was renamed Hotel Rival and opened for business on 1st September 2003.

"Our goal was to create a hotel with its own unique personality, the kind of place we would want to stay in ourselves," Benny said at the time. He had found that having stayed in hundreds of hotels all over the world, he only remembered a handful – the best and the worst. The aim of Hotel Rival is to create something much more memorable than the average hotel.

The hotel has 99 rooms with two of them having ABBA pictures on the walls. Each room also has a 32" plasma screen TV, DVD, CD player and a teddy bear! Sony Playstations are available from reception at no extra charge.

Mamma Mia! what a line-up! Benny, Pierce Brosnan, Amanda Seyfried, Meryl Streep, Agnetha, Frida, Christine Baranski, Colin Firth, writer Catherine Johnson, director Phyllida Lloyd, producer Judy Craymer, Björn and Dominic Cooper.

Hotel Rival is right on Mariatorget itself which is a picturesque square in a very lively part of the town. The area is a popular place for art galleries, fashion boutiques and bars.

With a whole new venue so close to his home and office at his disposal, Hotel Rival has increasingly become the venue for events that Benny is involved in.

In early 2006, he appeared on the Australian travel programme *The Great Outdoors* and showed the host, Ernie Dingo, around the hotel. He revealed that at that point, only one teddy bear had "been removed" from the hotel rooms!

The Cinema Rival was the venue for the Swedish première of *Mamma Mia! The Movie* on 4th July 2008 when all four members of ABBA were present. Frida, Benny and Björn all appeared separately on the red carpet and then Agnetha appeared suddenly from inside the hotel with Frida to surprise film star Meryl Streep. Frida led a dance on the red carpet with Agnetha and Meryl.

View of
RIDDARHOLMEN

20

Elva kvinnor i ett hus

Bastugatan 36

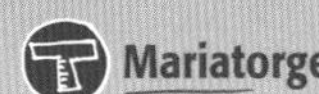

Mariatorget

43, 55

Agnetha released her Swedish solo album *Elva kvinnor i ett hus* (Eleven women in a house) in December 1975. It reached only no. 11 on the Swedish album charts, a disappointing position considering ABBA's success at the time. Agnetha composed all the tunes herself with words by Swedish lyricist Bosse Carlgren, the exception being the Swedish *SOS*, for which Stig Anderson wrote the lyrics and which was not originally intended for the album at all.

The album was recorded between 1974 and 1975 and was originally planned as a concept album featuring 12 songs – each one describing the differing circumstances of each of the women living in the house. The plan for twelve songs, including an elaborate gatefold sleeve for the album, was shelved when Agnetha had less and less time to devote to the project due to ABBA's immense success. Eleven songs were released on the album in the end.

The back cover photograph, taken by Ola Lager, featured the back of a white house. Ola had discovered the distinctive-looking building simply by driving around the southern part of Stockholm. He saw it, thought it could fit and took a shot. The front cover photo of Agnetha lying on some large cushions on a wooden floor was taken at Ola Lager's apartment at the time.

This house can be found at Bastugatan 36. To view the house as it is on the album cover, you should enter Lilla Skinnarviksgränd, a little road just off Bastugatan.

21

Kungliga Slottet

The Royal Palace
Slottsbacken 1

Gamla Stan
Kungsträdgården

2, 3, 43, 53

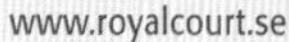

www.royalcourt.se

Kungliga Slottet is the biggest palace in the world that is still used by a head of state. It is King Carl XVI Gustav's official residence and is a daily place of work for The King and Queen of Sweden. The building, in baroque style, contains more than 600 rooms. The State Apartments with beautiful interiors from the 18th and 19th centuries are open to the public when not in use.

In 1975, ABBA took part in a photo-shoot for German electronics firm Blaupunkt posing in and around a car equipped with a Blaupunkt stereo. This photo session took place in Slottsbacken, the road leading up from Skeppsbron towards Storkyrkan and just to the south side of Kungliga Slottet.

On 8th March 1979, the four ABBA members along with Manager Stig Anderson and his wife Gudrun attended an official dinner at Kungliga Slottet hosted by the King and Queen. They found themselves mingling with high-profile politicians and business leaders.

On Friday 14th August 1992 a concert was held in the inner courtyard of Kungliga Slottet organised by *Artister för Miljö* (Artists for the Environment), an organisation founded by Frida. Its mission was to raise awareness of environmental issues through concerts and public appearances.

The concert was known as *Musik på Borggården* (Music on the courtyard). The King and the Queen were special guests, having given special permission for the event to be held on their premises. Frida herself gave her first live public

performance in 12 years and sang *What a Wonderful World* with Marie Fredriksson of Roxette, *Saltwater* (written by Julian Lennon) and *Änglamark* (Angel's ground) – an old Swedish classic song written by Evert Taube – with all the artists who performed that evening: Tomas Ledin, Marie Fredriksson and Håkan Hagegård.

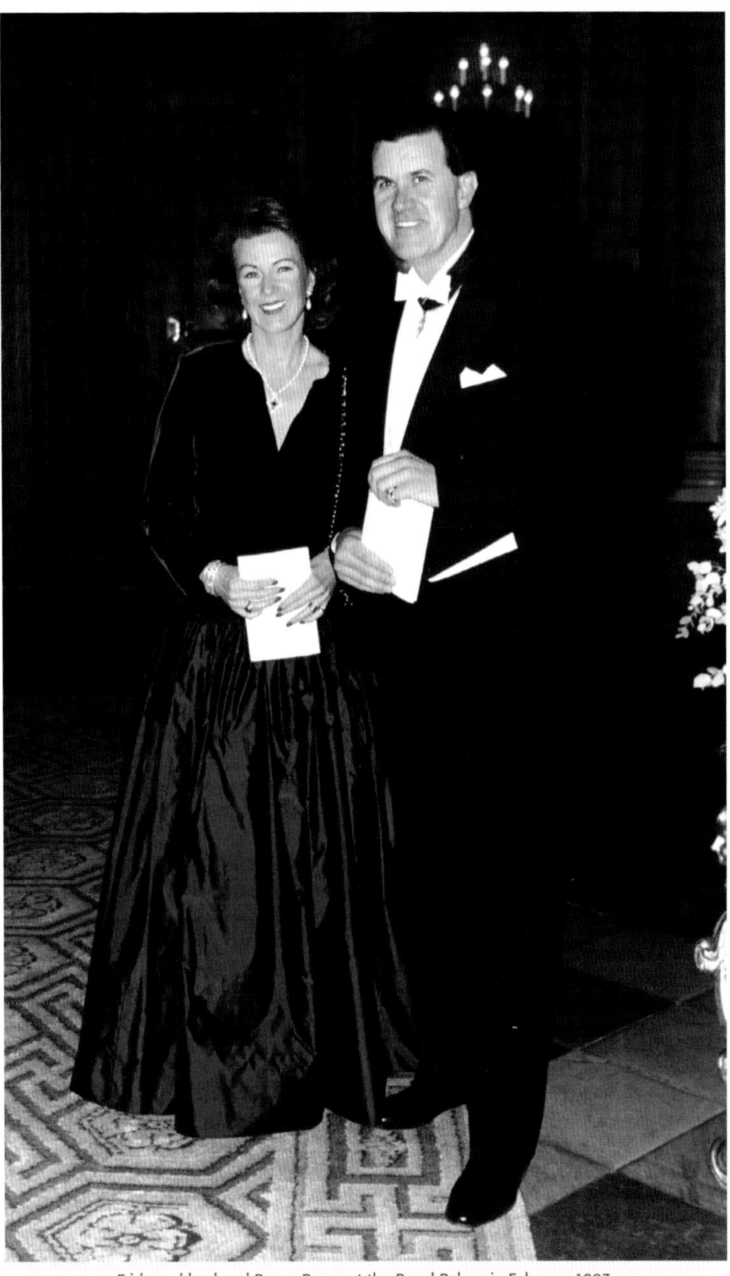

Frida and husband Ruzzo Reuss at the Royal Palace in February 1993.

At the many receptions held at Kungliga Slottet and hosted by the King and Queen, Frida was a frequent guest, being one of their close friends. Her husband from 1992–1999, Prince Ruzzo Reuss, was an old friend of the King.

Björn also attended some receptions here. In 1999, he was awarded the King's medal *Litteris Et Artibus* (Latin for Science and Art) – an award for special achievements within the fields of music, theatre and literature. He took his youngest daughter Anna along to the ceremony. In 2000, he and wife Lena attended the first official dinner of the year at Kungliga Slottet.

22

Skepps Bron

The Ship's Bridge
Skeppsbron

Gamla Stan
Kungsträdgården

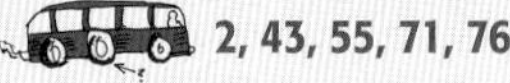
2, 43, 55, 71, 76

Skeppsbron is a long street and quay in Gamla Stan, overlooking the island of Skeppsholmen. The stone quay was not completed until 1854, so nowadays Skeppsbron refers to the road passing over the quay, while the harbour area outside of it is called Skeppsbrokajen. There is a large statue of King Gustav III just opposite Kungliga Slottet at the northern end of Skeppsbron.

In June 1999, ABBA's personal assistant and friend Görel Hanser celebrated her 50th birthday and held a big party, starting at the Moderna Museet (Museum of Modern Art) on Skeppsholmen followed by a boat trip from Gustav III's statue right next to the royal palace. All four ABBA members attended the party and even performed together, singing *Med en enkel tulipan* (With a simple tulip), apparently standing together on stage.

Having been offered one billion US dollars to reform and refusing it, they actually reformed and sang together for nothing – but it was for their friend, and in private. Anders Hanser, Görel's husband at the time, revealed at the ABBAMANIA event in Brighton in 2004, that the performance was photographed but that image will never be made public.

23

Västerlång Gatan

Western Long Street

 Gamla Stan  2, 3, 43, 53

Västerlånggatan is one of the longest streets in Gamla Stan and stretches virtually the whole length of the island. It follows the course of the city's 13th century defensive wall, which no longer exists. All along Västerlånggatan are restaurants, cafés, antique shops and boutiques.

During an extensive photo-shoot for the German teenage magazine BRAVO in 1974, Wolfgang "Bubi" Heilemann photographed ABBA around Stockholm including shopping and walking down Västerlånggatan.

In 1976, another photo session in Västerlånggatan took place, this time wearing thick fur coats. This was at the same time as the famous session at Stortorget (see p. 54).

24

Stor Torget

The Big Square

 Gamla Stan 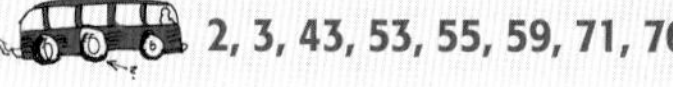 2, 3, 43, 53, 55, 59, 71, 76

Stortorget is a large public square in Gamla Stan with an iron well dating from 1778. It is today frequented by tens of thousands of tourists annually, and is occasionally the scene for demonstrations, performances, and renowned for its annual Christmas market offering traditional handicrafts and food.

One of ABBA's most famous photographs was taken next to the huge well on Stortorget with the marvellous coloured gabled buildings in the background. Björn stood with his toes on a grate so that you can pinpoint exactly where to stand to have your picture taken in the same spot!

To the right of the photograph as you look at it, is the former Stock Exchange building. Today it is the Nobel Museum.

Note: Agnetha was filmed cycling across Stortorget for her music video of her single *I Wasn't The One (Who Said Goodbye)* in 1987.

GAMLA STAN'S NARROWEST STREET.....

Frida and Benny's flat

Baggensgatan 21

 Gamla Stan 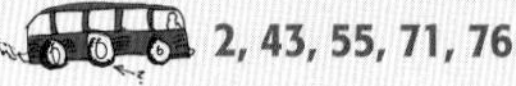 2, 43, 55, 71, 76

Frida and Benny moved from their home in Vallentuna in late 1975 to the top two floors of a luxurious maisonette in Gamla Stan. The apartment, in the cobbled street at Baggensgatan 21, could only be reached by climbing a 99-step winding staircase.

They welcomed TV cameras to their flat in 1976 when they filmed adverts for the Japanese electronics firm National. Four of the five commercials featured at least one scene from Frida and Benny's flat and were broadcast solely in Australia.

The commercials showed Benny using a vacuum cleaner while Frida was reading on the sofa lifting her feet so he wouldn't miss anything. Agnetha tried on headphones.

Benny was shown on the piano, turning the radio off as Frida approached so he could kiss her hand.

While filming the commercials, they also took the opportunity to film a short promotional film for movies on Channel 9 in Australia. In footage of *The Making Of The National Commercials* Agnetha and Frida were shown being made up in the kitchen; Benny is seen preparing a meal and they all sit in the courtyard outside the apartment's front door on benches while breaking for lunch. There is still a bench there today.

PLEASE NOTE!
This address has had (no) connection to ABBA since 1970s
please... respect the current tenants

Sundbergs Konditori
Sundbergs Konditori
CLICK!

26

The Iron Square

Järntorget is a small square in the southern part of Gamla stan, where the shopping streets Västerlånggatan and Österlånggatan meet. It is the second oldest square in Stockholm after Stortorget (see p. 54) dating back to around 1300.

In the middle of Järntorget is a cast iron well which was donated by the National Bank in 1829. In 1974, when ABBA walked around Gamla Stan for a photo session with German photographer Wolfgang "Bubi" Heilemann they posed around the well complete with guitar and banjo, pretending they were having a little jamming session. One of the pictures found its way onto one of some Swedish collector cards.

The well is now surrounded by tables and chairs belonging to a nearby café.

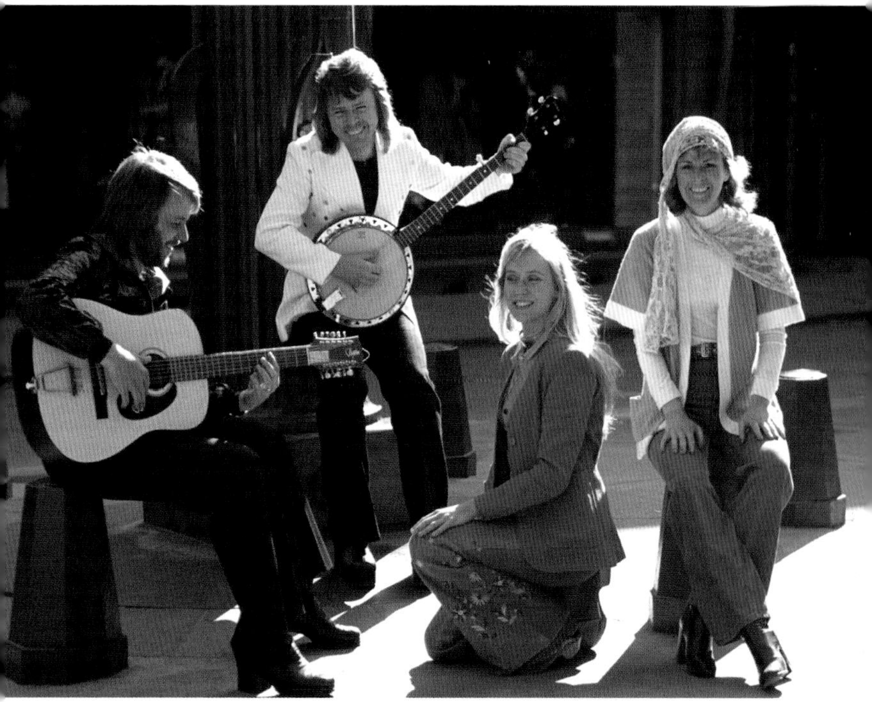

27

Evert Taubes Terrass

Evert Taube's Terrace on Riddarholmen

 Gamla Stan  3, 53, 59

Evert Taube was a Swedish musical composer and author (1890–1976). He was one of the most beloved and respected figures in the Swedish music history and has written many important works, including the environmentally minded *Änglamark,* a song which Frida performed at Kungliga Slottet in August 1992 (see p. 48).

The terrace area by the water on Riddarholmen that faces Stadshuset was named after Evert Taube. You can see a small statue of him playing the lute there.

The famous Lois Jeans photo session from late 1975 showing ABBA wearing Lois jeans and t-shirts was taken here with Stadshuset (see p. 40) in the background and just along the water's edge. One of the images found itself on the cover of the Australian and New Zealand release of the *Ring Ring* LP. Overall the images were widely used at the time, and some were included in an Australian bubble gum card set.

In the late summer of 1977, ABBA posed for the photo that ended up on the inner sleeve of *ABBA – The Album* which was released in December 1977 in Scandinavia. The same picture appeared on the back cover of the UK edition which was released in Spring 1978. It was taken on Evert Taubes Terrass at the point where the water's edge changes angles. You will know you have found the spot when you see a single tall chimney in the distance on Södermalm. To the right of that along the skyline you should see twin spires which belong to the Högalid church.

THE FAMOUS PHOTO SESSION
FOR LOIS JEANS....

For this photo-shoot ABBA also posed in front of Grand Hôtel (see p. 22).

28

Af Chapman

Flaggmansvägen 8

Djurgården Ferry from T Slussen  65 www.stfchapman.com

Af Chapman is a sailing ship, more than 120 years old. You cannot miss it as it is moored on the right-hand side as you arrive on Skeppsholmen. The ship was built in England in 1888. It sailed all over the world before being towed to Skeppsholmen by the Swedish Navy for permanent mooring as navy accommodation. Since the end of World War II, it has been a youth hostel which is open all year round. It has been refurbished just recently.

Being quite a symbol of Stockholm, it lent itself well as a background for photographs or filming.

In 1974, German photographer Wolfgang "Bubi" Heilemann took a fabulous shot of Benny and Björn carrying their respective partners in front of the ship, and it was featured again in February 1976 when Björn recorded some promotional trailers for Australian ABC TV's programme *Countdown.* Björn tells the viewers, *"And what about this boat here in Stockholm? It's even been to Australia you know."*

When Agnetha was interviewed for the American TV programme *Freeze Frame* in 1982, she gave some of her answers while sitting outside Bar Chapman, the café just opposite the boat. To the question, *"How long do you think ABBA's going to be together?"* she says, *"Oh, that's always hard to answer because I don't know. I think as long as the boys could write, we could go on forever!"*

Mono Music

Södra Brobänken 41A

Djurgården Ferry from  **Slussen**  **65**

www.monomusic.se

Heading to the south of Skeppsholmen, at the water's edge you'll find the offices of Mono Music. The company was founded in 1987 by Benny and Görel Hanser. It publishes music and also deals with more or less anything Benny finds himself being involved in. The offices were built in the 19th century and are a converted ship storage unit.

Mono Music Studios also reside here and is Scandinavia's finest mixing facility. Some of the world's biggest names in music have had their recordings completed at the studio. The first album release from Mono Music was Benny's 1987 album *Klinga mina klockor (Ring my bells).*

The offices are the central point for all ABBA-related business these days, and is also Görel's working base. Under the company name of Musik & Artist Service AB, Görel acts as the spokesperson for the group as well as the individual members, fending off press and fan enquiries on their behalf. She also represents various famous Swedish artists and Benny Anderssons Orkester (BAO!).

This is where Benny and Björn have their offices and Benny famously works 10am–5pm when he is in town. It is also the setting of many interviews Benny and Björn have given for TV programmes and specials. Frida sometimes drops in to visit when she is in Stockholm.

On 3rd July 2008, the day before the Swedish première of *Mamma Mia! The Movie,* Benny and Björn hosted a reception and press call at Mono Music where the guests mingled on the green lawn outside. They were photographed with the assembled cast of the movie at the beautiful waterfront overlooking Södermalm.

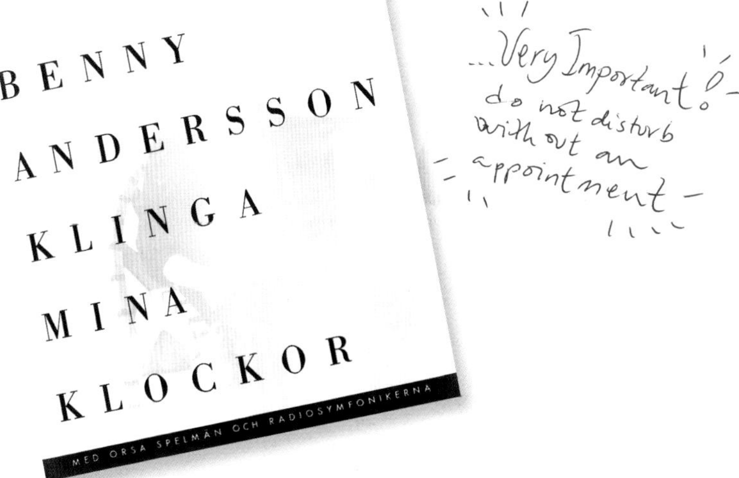

30

Paradiset

The Paradise
At the entrance to the Modern Museum

Djurgården Ferry from  **Slussen**  **65**

Paradiset is a collection of sixteen sculptures at the entrence to Moderna Museet. The sculptures, seven of which are made from iron, were created in 1966 by Niki de Saint Phalle from France and Jean Tinguely from Switzerland. They are easily found by heading through the centre of Skeppsholmen.

In 1974, German photographer Wolfgang "Bubi" Heilemann photographed ABBA in front of two of the sculptures. At the time the photographs were taken, the sculptures were closer to Skeppsholmsbron. They were moved to their current position near the entrance to Moderna Museet (Museum of Modern Art) in 1986 and sealed off, so you can no longer pose directly in front of them like ABBA did.

The nine brightly-coloured sculptures are made from plastic and fibreglass.

31

The Music Museum
Sibyllegatan 2

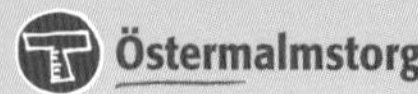

 62

www.musikmuseet.se

Located just behind Dramaten (The Royal Dramatic Theatre) at Nybroplan, Stockholm's Musikmuseet has been in existence for more than 100 years and has over 11,500 objects on display. Some of the exhibits in their musical instrument collection are hundreds of years old while others are brand new. Many of the instruments you are allowed to touch and some you can even play.

Thanks to the brainchild of German fan, Klaus-Peter Berg, there has been a small ABBA exhibition lurking three floors down in a corner of the museum since 9th February 1996.

Noticing on his first visit to Stockholm that there was no recognition for ABBA's musical achievements in their home town, he set out to put that right with the help of fellow German fan and founder of the ABBA fanzine *Intermezzo,* Regina Grafunder. It was she who contacted Musikmuseet with some proposals for an ABBA area in their building.

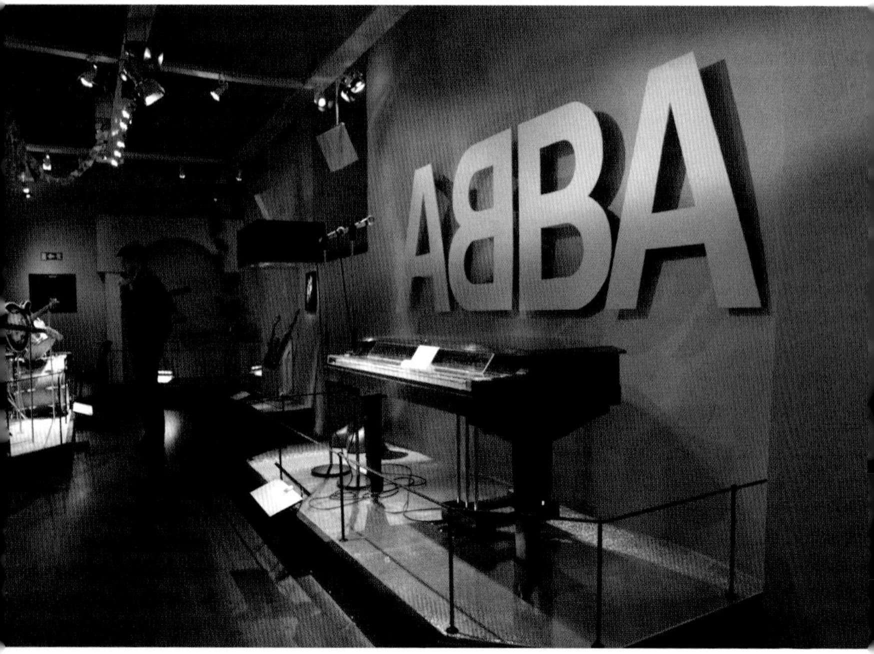

This little exhibition includes: Benny's Yamaha GS-1 synthesizer, gold discs of *The Visitors* from Austria, *Super Trouper* from Japan and *ABBA – The Singles, The First Ten Years* from Germany, a reconstruction of the ABBA logo with blinking lights (by Klaus-Peter Berg) and an "ABBA Information Computer" with a free ABBA Jukebox (*Dancing Queen* is the most requested song!). It has a database of more than 1,000 ABBA, solo and related records, tapes, CDs, books, videos and lyrics.

The ABBA exhibition is currently part of a collection called *Ensembles in Sweden – Man, Music, Environment* aiming to show visitors how music has been created and played in Sweden over the last 500 years, the ABBA section bringing things right up-to-date.

Castle Hotel

Now Hotel Riddargatan
Riddargatan 14

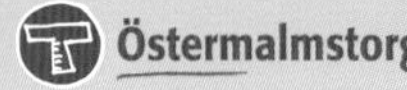
Östermalmstorg

62, 91

www.hotelriddargatan.se

The former Castle Hotel was a two star hotel a couple of blocks behind Dramaten (Royal Dramatic Theatre) and had 5 floors and 50 rooms.

The back cover picture of the *ABBA* album was taken in the reception area of the former Castle Hotel by photographer Ola Lager. The hotel has undergone at least one refurbishment since the picture was taken and now bears very little resemblance to the album shot.

The hotel was chosen because it had an old-fashioned 1930s feel to it and was in keeping with the style of the planned photo-shoot. The idea was to do something ironic in response to the huge criticism ABBA received at home in Sweden for being "too commercial" in the aftermath of their Eurovision win. ABBA were accused of being too "stuck-up" so why not show themselves like that for the next album? They wore costumes reminiscent of 1930s film stars.

Photographer Ola Lager wanted to use the existing lighting so ABBA could not move or laugh which luckily also suited the ironic theme of them having a "superior" attitude. The front cover picture of the album was taken on Tyrgatan (see p. 31) a couple of blocks from the Polar Music offices at the time (see p. 32).

"every song on the original album was released as either the A or a B side of a single somewhere in the world"

Frida & Benny's Apartments

Karlavägen 91 / Linnégatan 83
Karlaplan 3a

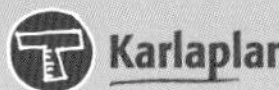

Karlaplan is an open park-plaza area in an exclusive area of Östermalm. Inspired by the star-shaped street patterns of Paris, Karlaplan was built in the late 19th century and is named in honour of all Swedish kings named Karl.

When Frida and Benny split up, Benny moved out of their villa on Lidingö to Karlavägen 91 close to Karlaplan and was living in the top two floors there by March 1981.

Meanwhile, Frida moved to an apartment at Linnégatan 83 not far from Karlaplan before moving to London at the end of 1982. The apartment was just around the corner from Historiska Museet (Museum of National Antiquities).

She was seen coming out of her front door and getting into her car in a TV documentary made during the recording of her first English language solo album *Something's Going On.* The album, produced by Phil Collins, was made during February and March 1982 at Polar Music Studios (see p. 34).

In Autumn 1984, Benny and his wife Mona moved a short distance to Karlaplan 3a where they lived in the top floor before moving to their current home.

PLEASE NOTE: These are private addresses that no longer have anything to do with ABBA. Please respect the privacy of the current residents.

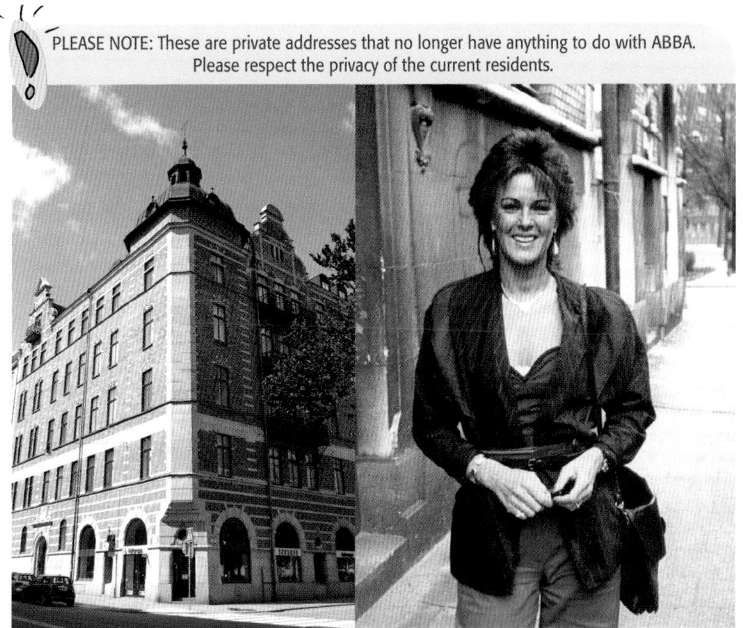

TV-Huset and SVT

Oxenstiernsgatan 26-34

Karlaplan

4

www.svt.se

TV-Huset is the headquarters of Sweden's national public broadcaster, broadcaster, SVT (Sveriges Television). Within their walls, ABBA recorded many, many TV programmes and appearances – here are some of the most memorable.

In 1973, *Melodifestivalen* was filmed at TV-Huset, the year when Agnetha, Benny, Björn and Anni-Frid finished third with *Ring Ring.* The following year, and now known as ABBA, they performed *Waterloo* in Swedish, won the competition and went on to win the 1974 Eurovision Song Contest in Brighton.

In May 1975 ABBA took part in the TV programme *Made In Sweden For Export* which show-cased current Swedish artists initially for broadcast to the Australian market. The other performers included singers Björn Skifs, Lill Lindfors and Sylvia Vrethammar who had a big European hit the previous year with *Y Viva España*. ABBA recorded performances of *Mamma Mia* and *So Long* at TV-Huset for this programme and this is where they wore the famous yellow and blue cat costumes for the first time.

During a break, photographer Bengt H Malmqvist, led them outside the front of the studio to take some new promotional shots. The session took just a few minutes before ABBA were called back inside for filming but the results have been very long-lasting with the image of Agnetha and Frida in the short cat costumes being used extensively ever since. A third performance of *I Do, I Do, I Do, I Do, I Do* was recorded later in the summer showing ABBA having a picnic and was included in the TV broadcast of *Made In Sweden For Export*.

In September 1976, the live concert part for the *ABBA-dabba-dooo!!* special was filmed here. ABBA performed three songs. Two of them were live, raw and fantastic – *Dum Dum Diddle* and *Why Did It Have To Be Me?* – while a mimed performance of *Money, Money, Money* turned out to be one of the most played performances on TV, especially in Australia.

In the final scene of the film *ABBA – The Movie* the band members were in an elevator when DJ Ashley, who had been chasing over Australia trying to get an interview with them, happened to walk in on them. The doors closed and ABBA sang *Eagle*. The song was portrayed in the film as being performed entirely inside the elevator. In the TV studios where it was filmed, the elevator was quite a few feet off the ground so ABBA had to climb up a ladder to reach it. Agnetha was pregnant with Christian at the time, so extra special care had to be taken as she climbed up.

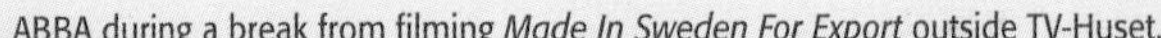

ABBA during a break from filming *Made In Sweden For Export* outside TV-Huset.

ONE of The final scenes
ABBA – The Movie

In 1980, ABBA had to record an appearance for German TV programme *Show Express* in Stockholm after Agnetha and Björn received threats to kidnap their children. They cancelled their trip to Germany, so the producers of the show came to Sweden instead. They flew over their crew, technicians and even the set!

From 27th – 29th April 1981, ABBA were back at Sveriges Television to record the TV special *Dick Cavett Meets ABBA* consisting of an interview with American show host Dick Cavett and a live mini-concert complete with their band. They performed nine songs including a couple from their most recent album *Super Trouper* and their forthcoming album *The Visitors,* plus a handful of old favourites. Some of these live performances were included in the album *ABBA Live,* released in 1986.

The last ever public performance by ABBA as a group was filmed here for the British TV programme *The Late, Late Breakfast Show* where they performed *I Have A Dream* and *Under Attack* to playback. In between the songs each ABBA member was interviewed by host Noel Edmonds.

The last ever public performance by ABBA as a group.

35

Ladugårds Gärdet

The Barn's Field

69 Källhagen

Ladugårdsgärdet, meaning the barn's field, is a large open grassy area in northern Djurgården, also known as Gärdet. It is located just across the road from Sjöhistoriska Museet (see p. 80).

ABBA were photographed sitting on a Swedish flag with the 155m high Kaknästornet (Kaknäs Tower) in the background in 1972. Kaknästornet is the hub of all radio and TV transmissions in Sweden. Views from the top of the tower are spectacular. There is a restaurant and a gift shop. The tower has one of the fastest elevator rides in the world.

Pictures from this photo session were used in 1973 on the *Ring Ring* single in West Germany and on the white label promo single of *Another Town, Another Train* from Japan.

During filming for *ABBA – The Movie,* Frida appeared in a photograph throwing a frisbee during rehearsals at Ladugårdsgärdet, also with Kaknästornet in the distance.

Kaknäs Tower

36

Sjöhistoriska Museet

The National Maritime Museum
Djurgårdsbrunnsvägen 24

69 Källhagen

www.sjohistoriska.se

Sjöhistoriska Museet tells the story of merchant shipping, naval defence and ship-building in Sweden. Their collection ranges from the 16th century gold-ornamented naval warships through to 19th century clippers and steamships right up to the submarines and oil tankers of today.

In autumn 1975, ABBA were photographed standing in front of the big green iron doors of the museum. Pictures from this photo session were used extensively around the world at the time and showed up on two different sets of bubble gums cards, one from Australia and one from the Netherlands.

Note that during the museum's opening hours, you might be hard pressed to get a decent photo with the doors shut because they tend to remain open all day.

Here, ABBA also posed on a cannon which is situated around the back of the museum near the car park. The cannon has been moved since then and whilst not very often, is subject to being moved at any time.

The photos at Sjöhistoriska Museet were taken on the same day as both the under the autumn tree (see p. 86) and park bench sessions (see p. 88), which produced the cover of the *Greatest Hits* album.

37

Stig's Grave

Galärvarvskyrkogården
Djurgårdsvägen

Djurgården Tram 7  **44, 47**

ABBA's Manager, Stig Erik Leopold Anderson, died on 12th September 1997.

His funeral service took place at Sankt Jacobs kyrka in central Stockholm (see p. 15) on Friday 10th October 1997 and he was laid to rest in a private family burial a week later.

Stig's family grave is in a little cemetery called Galärvarvskyrkogården, situated just behind Nordiska Museet (The Nordic Museum) and next to Vasamuseet (The Vasa Museum). The cemetery has been there since 1742 and has approximately 1,300 burial plots. At the same site, there is a national monument to the 852 people who died in the Estonia ferry tragedy in 1994.

Stig has a simple grave with a grey marble surround and an area for flowers in the middle. The first line of the headstone features the musical symbol of a treble clef. The grave is in the middle of the section lying to the north of the main cemetery path, opposite the chapel. As you stand facing the grave, Nordiska Museet will be on your right.

38

Ulla Winbladh

Rosendalsvägen 8

Djurgården Tram 7  **44, 47**

www.ullawinbladh.se

The restaurant Ulla Winbladh was built in 1897. It became a restaurant in the 1950s after originally being a bakery. Its name, Ulla Winbladh, was the "poetic name" of Maria Kristina Källström, one of the mistresses of Sweden's beloved poet and composer, Bellman. It has a very distinctive and unusual high red-tiled roof and sits in the shadow of Skansen (see p. 94).

In autumn 1975, ABBA were pictured outside the restaurant, which was one of the locations used for a photo session that became synonymous with the *Greatest Hits* shoot taken by photographer Bengt H Malmqvist. One of the shots taken outside the restaurant ended up on one of three Australian merchandise wall scrolls.

In summer 1976 ABBA posed again outside the restaurant, this time around a table and also with and Frida and Agnetha sitting on the grass. If you look closely at the Frida and Agnetha shot, you can see Benny and Björn sitting at one of the tables in the distance! The group table shot was taken with them facing the restaurant. The photo made it onto an Australian jigsaw puzzle.

The restaurant has since expanded beyond the brick walls and has a covered outside dining area enclosed by a picket fence. The main building is still intact and its roof design is instantly recognizable.

39

Under the Autumn Tree

Rosendalsvägen

Djurgården Tram 7  **44, 47**

As part of the photo session taken by Bengt H Malmqvist that resulted in photos being used for the *Greatest Hits* album, some under the autumn tree shots were taken very close to Ulla Winbladh restaurant (see p. 84) where there are lots of trees. The pictures were taken around mid-day even though the lighting looks like it's towards the end of the day with the sun low in the sky.

Like the park bench photo session (see p. 88), the exact location of the tree in question is unsure. It is within 50m of the restaurant Ulla Winbladh according to Bengt H Malmqvist.

There is a lone tree on the corner of the green area right next to Ulla Winbladh. The photograph indicates a low hedge and road in the background like the original photographs, so the pictures may very well have been taken under this tree.

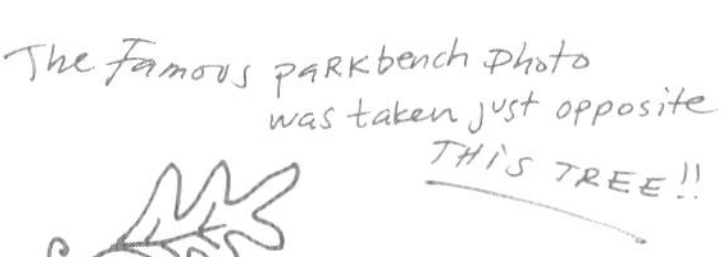

Park bench Photo session

Rosendalsvägen

Djurgården Tram 7  **44, 47**

Probably one of the most famous and iconic photo sessions ABBA ever did was the park bench photo session. Photographer Bengt H Malmqvist was just taking some publicity shots. *"I had known them quite a while, knew them very well, we spent a couple of hours moving around Djurgården,"* he said. These pictures were taken the same day as those at Ulla Winbladh (see p. 84), Sjöhistoriska Museet (see p. 80) and under the autumn tree (see p. 86).

The park bench session worked out so well that one of the shots ended up as the cover for the *Greatest Hits* album in the UK, USA, Canada and Italy. The fact that Agnetha looked so sad in the pictures was intentional. It was supposed to portray Agnetha and Björn in a different mood to the other couple. As Bengt described, *"Agnetha was trying to show she was perhaps waiting for a kiss herself."* And what a kiss! The *Greatest Hits* cover shows Frida and Benny kissing and holding hands. Further photos in the session show Benny's hand rising to Frida's shoulder and then her hand disappearing under his jacket. One picture, released in black and white in the *Greatest Hits* music folio, shows Frida and Benny almost lying backwards on the bench.

Agnetha's sadness at not being on the receiving end of a kiss like Frida's was just for the cameras however, as other pictures in the session have her and Björn looking up and smiling.

The park bench was just 50m from the Ulla Winbladh restaurant on Djurgården. However, it's over 30 years since the pictures were taken and benches can be moved or removed, bushes can be cut down and paths can be resurfaced. Luckily large trees do not change that much in 30 years and the key feature of the park bench session pictures is that of a tree with a slight slant to the right. There is such a tree with the same bark markings along the road just before the Ulla Windbladh with a car park behind it, but no sign of a bench in front of it.

Cirkus

Djurgårdsslätten 43-45

Djurgården Tram 7  **44, 47**

www.cirkus.se

Situated on Djurgården since 1892, the theatre was, as the name would suggest, originally used as a circus arena. Today it is mainly used for concerts, theatre and musical shows. In recent years, Cirkus has seen several appearances by ABBA members, both individually and together.

ABBA recorded the TV show *Nygammalt* (New & Old) in December 1974 which was broadcast on National Swedish Television on 3rd January 1975. They performed *I've Been Waiting For You* and *So Long* and were interviewed. Unfortunately the only existing footage of this appearance is a portion of *I've Been Waiting For You.*

On 17th February 1997, at the Swedish Grammys, Benny was awarded Composer of the Year, and the soundtrack of the musical *Kristina Från Duvemåla* was awarded Album of the Year. Benny announced that the stage production would hit Cirkus in Stockholm the following year.

Kristina Från Duvemåla opened at Cirkus on 14th February 1998. There wasn't a venue big enough in Stockholm, so Cirkus was given a major overhaul for the production – Sweden's largest ever musical! It started its run in Malmö and then Gothenburg while the building work took place in Stockholm.

The main players in Kristina Från Duvemåla – Stockholm, February 1998. Back row left to right: Director Lars Rudolfson, Benny and Björn. Front row: Helen Sjöholm (Kristina), Anders Ekborg (Karl-Oskar), Åse Bergh (Ulrika) and Peter Jöback (Robert).

On 17th August 1998, all four ABBA members were together at Cirkus for the 50th birthday celebrations of EMA-Telstar concert promoter Thomas Johansson, who was ABBA's tour organiser in both 1977 and 1979. He is briefly featured in *ABBA – The Movie.*

In 1999, Benny and Björn were interviewed by the Observer Magazine and described the event: *"About a year ago, a friend of ours had his 50th birthday and all four of us were under the same roof for the first time since 1981 or 1982* [in fact it was January 1986]. *Afterwards I thought to myself, 'Oh my God, this hasn't happened before! What if we had all arrived together?' I never thought Agnetha would show up, but it was all comfortable. We get along really well. We didn't exactly stand chatting, the four of us. No – two and two maybe. Never four. Of course I feel an emotional tie to the other three. When one has gone through such a fantastic thing together, there is something very special; no one else can ever have it. For that reason, maybe we should all get together over dinner or something. Very few people in this world have gone through what we did together."*

The final performance of *Kristina Från Duvemåla* was on Saturday 19th June 1999 to a capacity audience of more than 650 people. Both Benny and Björn were there with the main stars, Helen Sjöholm, Peter Jöback and Anders Ekborg, who all made sure they were available to star in the last performance. The long-awaited Swedish production of *Chess* opened at Cirkus on 23rd February 2002. Benny and Björn attended the première with lyricist Tim Rice. The show ran until 15th June 2003.

Björn and Benny with lyricist Tim Rice at Cirkus.

The morning after a Rolling Stones concert at Cirkus on 22nd July 2003, ABBA fans all over the world were stunned to see that Agnetha had attended. She sat in the VIP area next to Per Gessle and Marie Fredriksson from Roxette. Two photographs emerged of her looking stunning, waving and smiling. After three years with no new pictures, this was a rare treat. A friend told newspaper Aftonbladet, *"The Rolling Stones is one of Agnetha's absolute favourite bands. She was looking forward to this concert and got tickets through her contacts a long time in advance."*

The première of the Swedish production of *Mamma Mia!* took place at Cirkus on 12th February 2005.

This was a very special evening because all four ABBA members were there although they didn't appear together at any point. Frida and Agnetha sat on separate sides of the auditorium and applauded as Benny and Björn took the applause on stage with the cast.

The final performance of *Mamma Mia!* in Stockholm at Cirkus was on the 7th January 2007. A surprise guest was Agnetha who showed up with a friend. Benny and Björn both took to the stage for the curtain call. Agnetha attended the after-show party and sang the duet *True Love* with Tommy Körberg. She also joined in another song on stage standing next to Björn.

ABBA fans across the world were surprised and delighted to wake up to the news on 24th January 2009 that Agnetha and Frida had attended the annual Rockbjörnen (Rock Bear) awards at Cirkus the night before and took to the stage to accept a Lifetime Achievement diploma on behalf of ABBA. They were interviewed live for several minutes.

Skansen

Djurgårdsslätten 49–51

Djurgården Tram 7  **44, 47**

www.skansen.se

Founded in 1891, Skansen is the oldest open-air museum in the world with approximately 150 buildings brought from all over Sweden, dating back to the 18th and 19th centuries. Most of the buildings are open and there are guides dressed in traditional costumes doing old-fashioned crafts such as weaving, butter-making, spinning, etc. There are open-air concerts regularly on summer evenings and fabulous views of the city. There is also a zoo and lots of ABBA-related things to see.

Towards the rear of Skansen you can find Kronbergs Ateljé (Kronberg's studio) featuring the artwork of painter Julius Kronberg (1850–1921.) He was a professor at the Royal Swedish Academy of Arts. His works feature at Kungliga Slottet (see p. 48), the Hallwyl Palace and Dramaten. After his death, his studio was donated to Nordiska Museet but later moved to Skansen.

Kronberg's painting of *Eros* is on the cover of ABBA's album *The Visitors.* Everything is still almost as it was in 1981 in the studio. Look out for the book that Agnetha is flicking through and the wooden bench that Benny sits on. Unfortunately you won't be allowed to sit on it as it has been roped off for some time. The red armchair that Frida sits on can be found in the room away from the painting. Keep looking and you'll find it. You'll notice that there is a large water stain on it that Frida obscures by sitting in front of it for the album cover! The chair that Björn is leaning against is also in the room. On the wall opposite the large window you will find the collection of small paintings in frames that featured on the reverse of the album cover.

Some alternative versions of the cover picture have Agnetha wearing a coat and Björn sitting on the wooden bench instead of Benny.

Apparently ABBA contacted Kronberg's family to ask permission to use the image on the album cover. Kronberg's son approved the plan on condition that a copy of the album cover would be sent to him when the album was released. No record, just the album cover!

Kronberg's painting of Eros is on the cover of ABBA's album *The Visitors*.

Seeing this for the first time is a magical experience. Note that flash photography is not permitted in the room. Kronbergs Ateljé is not open on a daily basis. If you're lucky, you might find it open, especially in August, otherwise you can ask one of the staff who are usually happy to let you in – they are used to ABBA fans asking to see it.

Lill-Skansen is just around the corner, slightly north from Kronbergs Ateljé. It is a children's zoo and playground area with masses of small animals. At the back of it after walking all the way around the outside you'll find a giant red wooden Dala horse in a sandpit play area. Benny and Björn had a photo session in 1972 with this Dala horse. One of the pictures was used for the 1972 single release of *En Carousel* backed with *Lycka* in Japan. The single cover actually featured inaccurate song titles! The tracks featured on the discs were *Merry-Go-Round* and *Tänk om jorden vore ung* (What if the world was young). The current Dala horse has been repainted, so it doesn't have exactly the same design as Benny and Björn's one.

A Dalecarlian horse or Dala horse – in Swedish "Dalahäst" – is a traditional wooden carving of a horse originating from the Swedish province of Dalarna. It was originally made as a children's toy, but nowadays it is widely used as a symbol for Sweden. They are traditionally painted bright red with a harness and other details in white, green, yellow and blue. The distinctive shape of the horse is due to flat-plane carving. The horses were originally made of the scrap wood from the clock case industry in the Dalarna region.

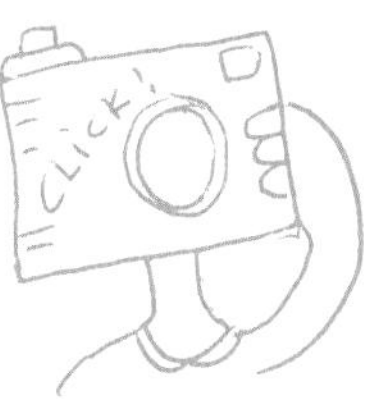

ABBA members have performed at Skansen many, many times over the years on the various stages at Skansen. Perhaps though the most important was Frida's performance on 3rd September 1967 on the Solliden stage. She had just won the *Nya ansikten* (New faces) competition there after which, as part of her prize, she was whisked off to the TV studios to perform live as a guest on a special edition of the popular TV show *Hylands hörna* (Hyland's corner), Frida performed her winning song *En ledig dag* (A day off).

In 1975, both Agnetha and Frida took part in the summer TV series of 1975 *Sommarnöjet* (Summer entertainment) although their performances were a few weeks apart. On 2nd August 1975, Agnetha sang *Dom har glömt* (They have forgotten) and *Tack för en underbar vanlig dag* (Thank you for a wonderful ordinary day) live from her solo album *Elva kvinnor i ett hus* (see p. 47). Her backing vocalists were brother and sister Anders and Karin Glenmark, who went on to perform on the album *Chess* and then became the duo *Gemini* in the 1980s, produced by Benny and Björn. Frida's performance was on 28th August 1975. She sang *Syrtaki* and *Aldrig mej* (Never me) from her solo album *Frida ensam* (Frida alone).

Swedish midsummer, a tradition at Skansen.

In recent years, Benny has been a regular performer on the popular summer TV series *Allsång på Skansen* (Sing-a-long at Skansen). He backed Helen Sjöholm on accordion in 1997 and, since the formation of Benny Anderssons Orkester (BAO!) in 2001, he has performed annually (with notable absences in 2006 and 2009). In 2001, Björn was in the audience with wife Lena when Helen Sjöholm and Josefin Nilsson performed *Jag vet vad han vill*, the Swedish version of the *Chess* number *I Know Him So Well.*

Enjoy the wonderful views from Skansen.

Explore Skansen's old houses....

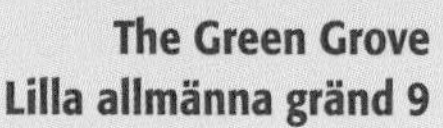

Gröna Lund

The Green Grove
Lilla allmänna gränd 9

Djurgården Tram 7  **44, 47**

www.gronalund.com

Established in 1883, Tivoli Gröna Lund is an amusement park located virtually opposite one of the entrances to Skansen. Compared to other amusement parks it is relatively small due to its city centre location which has meant that expansion has been limited. However, it still manages to cover 38,000m^2 and welcomes over a million visitors every year. Gröna Lund is also a popular venue for concerts on summer evenings and has welcomed Jimi Hendrix, Paul McCartney and Bob Marley in its time. It features most attractions you usually find in amusement parks for both big and little kids including a Haunted House, Tunnel of Love and the most popular rides of all – the roller-coasters. There is also a plentiful supply of gift shops, snack bars and restaurants.

Gröna Lund is mentioned in two solo Agnetha songs. Firstly there's a line in her 1975 song *Gulleplutt* (the English version was called *Golliwog*) and also in her 1987 single *På söndag* (On Sunday) sung with her son Christian.

On Sunday 3rd September 1967 The Hootenanny Singers were completing their latest Folkpark tour with two concerts at Gröna Lund, one in the afternoon and one in the evening. This is the date that Sweden switched from driving on the left to the right and as The Hootenanny Singers performed the second show on stage at Gröna Lund, Frida was winning the *Nya ansikten* (New faces) competition at Skansen, just a few hundred metres away (see p. 94).

On 30th June 1975, ABBA appeared in concert on the main stage, called Stora Scenen, as part of their Swedish Folkpark tour. Attendance was good – they broke crowd numbers at the time for a Swedish pop act with 19,200 people all of whom had to pay on the gate as no tickets were sold in advance. Consequently Stockholm city centre experienced significant traffic snarl-ups.

Photos taken at this concert, showing ABBA with incredible energy, found their way onto the cover of the *Money, Money, Money* single in some territories.

A very famous picture of ABBA was taken at Gröna Lund with ABBA holding hands and running in front of the giant ferris wheel. They were actually running across the area in front of Stora Scenen.

The picture was used for the inside cover of the French *Golden Double* album released in 1976 and one of the three merchandise cloth wall hangings from Australia. It also featured on Australian bubble gum cards. Unfortunately, with the lack of space available at Gröna Lund for new rides, the ferris wheel was replaced in 2007 with a small roller-coaster ride called Kvasten.

Around the same time (1976), ABBA were pictured in front of one of the attractions armed with a couple of Snoopy look-a-like cuddly toys.

ABBA
money, money, money

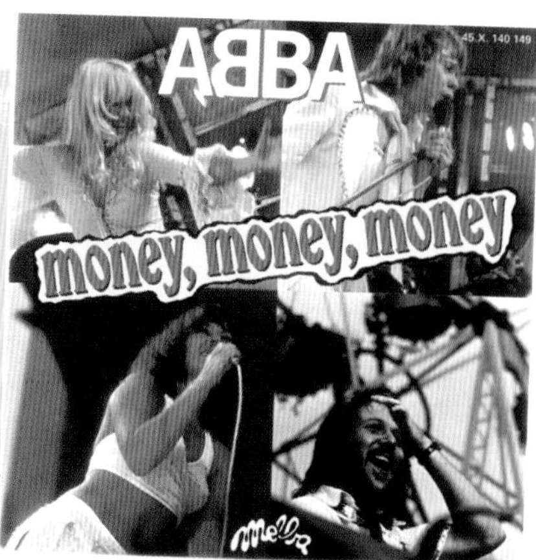
45.X. 140 149
ABBA
money, money, money

FAIRGROUND FROLIC–
FAIRGROUND FROLIC—STOCKHOLM
No. 45 of 72 B

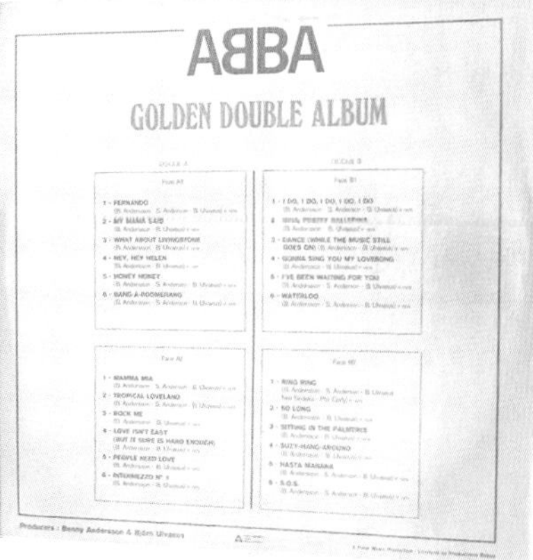
ABBA
GOLDEN DOUBLE ALBUM
1 - FERNANDO
2 - MY MAMA SAID
3 - WHAT ABOUT LIVINGSTONE
4 - HEY, HEY HELEN
5 - HONEY HONEY
6 - BANG-A-BOOMERANG
1 - I DO, I DO, I DO, I DO, I DO
2 - NINA, PRETTY BALLERINA
3 - DANCE (WHILE THE MUSIC STILL GOES ON)
4 - GONNA SING YOU MY LOVESONG
5 - I'VE BEEN WAITING FOR YOU
6 - WATERLOO
1 - MAMMA MIA
2 - TROPICAL LOVELAND
3 - ROCK ME
4 - LOVE ISN'T EASY (BUT IT SURE IS HARD ENOUGH)
5 - PEOPLE NEED LOVE
6 - INTERMEZZO N° 1
1 - RING RING
2 - SO LONG
3 - SITTING IN THE PALMTREE
4 - SUZY-HANG-AROUND
5 - HASTA MAÑANA
6 - S.O.S.
Producers: Benny Andersson & Björn Ulvaeus

Villa Ekarne
Singelbacken 21

 **47 Ryssviksvägen**

ABBA's Manager, Stig Anderson, lived at Villa Ekarne from October 1977 until late 1984 when he and his wife Gudrun divorced. By the early 1990s he had moved back in with his ex-wife until the house was sold in 1996. Villa Ekarne was designed in 1905 by architect Ragnar Östberg, who amongst other projects went on to design Stadshuset (see p. 40) in 1923.

It was here on 25th January 1981 that all four ABBA members took part in a surprise party for Stig's 50th birthday. They arrived at 7am and continued to celebrate throughout the day. Benny and Björn, armed with an accordion, made their entrance up a ladder and onto the balcony outside the bedroom where they then sang specially-written lyrics to the tune of *Ljuva sextital* (Good old sixties), which they had written with Stig in 1969.

Stig was also treated to a song and dance routine by the wives and girlfriends of some of the key Polar Music personnel including Agnetha, Frida, Görel Hanser and Björn's new wife Lena. Later in the day, as part of a three-part video show, *Salute to Stig (Hovas vittne)* (Salute to Stig (Hova's witness)), featuring ABBA wearing their Eurovision Song Contest costumes was shown. This had been recorded the day before at the entertainment venue Berns and was a specially-written song for Stig's birthday.

NOTE: This address no longer has any connection to ABBA. Please respect the current owners.

People Need Love
Rain shelter

Rosendalsvägen/de Besches väg

 **69 Djurgårdsbrunn**

In 1970 Benny, Björn, Agnetha and Anni-Frid were photographed under a rain shelter and one of the pictures in the session appeared on the cover of the Polar single *People Need Love* in 1972. It was quite an extensive photo session as they appear to have been photographed from every possible angle.

The rain shelter is still there, tucked away at the top of southern Djurgården. It can be found just to the right as you pass over Djurgårdsbrunnsbron from north Djurgården. It is located between Rosendalsvägen and de Besches väg. Ask the bus driver to tell you when you get to Djurgårdsbrunn bus stop.

46

Djurgårds Kanalen

The Djurgården canal
Djurgårdsbron/Manillavägen

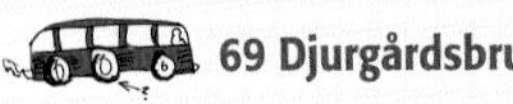 **69 Djurgårdsbrunn**

Building of Djurgårdskanalen was completed in 1934, nine years after it began. A stroll by the water is truly idyllic.

In *ABBA – The Movie* there is a sequence during *The Name Of The Game* where character DJ Ashley dreams he is close friends with ABBA. We see him enjoying their company in various scenarios. One of those, although it only lasts a few seconds on screen, is a boat trip with Agnetha and Frida worshipping at his feet while Benny and Björn look on. That scene was filmed on the Djurgården canal just to the left of the bridge Djurgårdsbrunnsbron, heading away from the city in the summer of 1977.

A short scene from *The Name Of The Game* in *ABBA – The Movie*.

Scenes from *ABBA – The Movie* were filmed in the green area just south of Djurgården canal, including those involving the photographers, Ashley and Frida's hug, the golf scene and some dream sequences for the tune *The Name Of The Game*.

Frida and Benny were photographed in front of a very distinctive 'V' shaped tree with the canal just behind them. The tree is just across Djurgårdsbrunnsbron on the road Manillavägen when heading south. It is the fourth tree on the left opposite a small recycling depot. In fact if you look to the right, you should be able to see the *People Need Love* rain shelter (see p. 106) in the distance.

AGNETHA IN A BREAK FROM FILMING
SCENES FOR THE DREAM SEQUENCE
IN ABBA – THE MOVIE!

Globen

Now Ericsson Globe
Globentorget 2

Globen

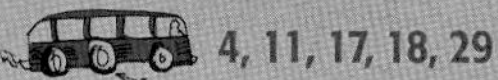
4, 11, 17, 18, 29

www.globearenas.se

Situated two miles south of central Stockholm and shaped like a huge golfball, the Ericsson Globe, also known as Globen, opened in 1989 and is currently the largest spherical building in the world, boasting an audience capacity of 16,000 spectators for shows and concerts. In 2010 Sweden's latest tourist attraction SkyView opened here. A glass capsule takes brave visitors upwards around the curved edge of the building to the top of Globen, 130 metres above sea level. Enjoy the most impressive sight of the city!

Benny and Björn joined U2 on stage for *Dancing Queen* on 11th June 1992 on the band's final night at Globen during their European *ZOOTV* Tour.

Globen was the venue for three very special B&B Tribute Concerts on 30th and 31st October and 1st November 1998. The concerts featured nothing but songs written by Benny and Björn. The Gothenburg Symphony Orchestra was led by Anders Eljas while the rock band consisted of ABBA musicians Rutger Gunnarsson, Per Lindvall and Lasse Wellander. The performers were Karin and Anders Glenmark, Tommy Körberg, Helen Sjöholm and Orsa Spelmän. It was at this event that Helen Sjöholm first performed *Money, Money, Money.*

From left to right: Tommy Körberg, Karin Glenmark, Helen Sjöholm and Anders Glenmark

The backdrop on the stage was two enormous back-to-back 'B's and when the ABBA section started, two giant 'A's appeared at either end while the crowd went into a frenzy!

On 31st October 1998 Benny joined the performers on stage – he just strolled on stage and was handed a spare accordion. He said a few words about the last time he had played at Globen together with U2 and then joined Orsa Spelmän for a lively rendition of *Födelsedagsvals till Mona* (Birthday waltz for Mona). Benny sprinted onto the stage from his seat in the audience when the ABBA section started with *Take A Chance On Me!* In the papers the following morning, Benny was quoted as saying, *"It felt fantastic. It was rock'n'roll, something that ABBA weren't that good at. It feels rather fascinating that there is life in the old work. I can't grasp how big ABBA were."*

To celebrate 30 years of ABBA, three concerts were staged at Globen from 22nd – 24th August 2002 entitled *ABBA The Tribute – The 30th Anniversary Show.* More than 20,000 tickets were sold in under two days.

On Friday 26th October 2007 Benny Anderssons Orkester (BAO!) along with Helen Sjöholm and Tommy Körberg performed in Globen. The arena was transformed into a dance hall for the occasion and they presented the first live performance of Benny and Björn's composition *Crush On You* written during the ABBA years, but never intended for ABBA to record.

48

Hovet Isstadion

Ice Stadium

Globentorget 2, Johanneshov

www.globearenas.se

Originally known as Johanneshov's Sport Arena in the 1920s, this giant venue in the shadow of its close neighbour Globen is today known as Hovet (The Court). It is Sweden's largest indoor ice hockey rink, but also stages concerts and corporate events, holding a seating capacity of 9,800 people.

For one night only on 20th October 1979, ABBA performed live in concert at Isstadion as part of their North American and European Tour. They got a rapturous reception from the home audience. Benny is quoted as saying, *"You might wonder what the hell you're doing in the USA when it's like this at home."* Queen Silvia attended the concert with Princess Lillian and met ABBA after the show, getting their autographs and went home with some ABBA goodies.

49

Lidingö

Island north east of Stockholm

Lidingö is a large island situated to the north-east of central Stockholm. It is a residential area where many wealthy people live. House prices are above average.

Between November 1976 and December 1980, all four ABBA members lived on Lidingö at the same time either as couples or as individuals. Agnetha and Björn lived there for virtually the whole of the ABBA years in various properties.

Agnetha and Björn moved from Vallentuna (see p. 135) to Strandstigen 4 in October 1974 close to Millesgården, the home and studio of the sculptor Carl Milles, Lidingö's most famous tourist attraction. Their back garden overlooked the Lidingö bridge and had the local train line at the foot of the garden.

November 1976 saw a lot of house-moving activity in the ABBA camp – quite incredible considering their workload at the time. They had recently completed promotional trips to the USA and Canada and completed a TV special in Poland. In November 1976 the *Arrival* album was released and there were promotional trips to England, the Netherlands and France.

The Ulvaeus family at their first Lidingö home.

Frida and Benny moved out of the apartment in Gamla Stan (see p. 56) in November 1976 and into a large house at Södra Kungsvägen 241 in the Käppala area of Lidingö. The house, also known as "The Pink Villa", had been used in 1969 for the Swedish film *Miss and Mrs Sweden.*

At one time Benny's son Peter and Frida's son Hans also lived there. The house was full of instruments and Benny had a studio in the basement with lots of equipment.

In November 1976 Agnetha and Björn moved to Västra Allén 12A on the corner of Trädgårdsvägen, in the Käppala area, after two years in their first Lidingö home.

As always, filming of ABBA videos and programmes was done in nearby convenient locations. The outdoor snow scene in the music video for *Knowing Me, Knowing You* in early 1977 was filmed in a local park on Lidingö.

Agnetha and Björn moved again in October 1977, after less than a year, because *"the location of the house was too open"* and *"the most excited fans just walked straight in".* They moved to Björkuddsstranden 6, not too far away from Frida and Benny.

It was here that the music video for *The Name Of The Game* was filmed in the kitchen and in the garden – where a roundabout was brought in for one of the outside effects. Records show that the recording of this video took place in September 1977 so perhaps they filmed it before they moved in properly.

Frida and Benny married after a nine-year engagement on 6th October 1978 at the Lidingö kyrka, a small Lutheran church from 1623, beautifully situated by the water at Kyrkviken (Church Bay). It was an intimate and private ceremony as they had hardly told anyone they were getting married. The only witnesses were the verger and their house-keeper Bitte. To make up for this, they held a party at their house the following day.

Agnetha moved out of her and Björn's house at Christmas 1978. She moved to Jupitervägen 12A back in the Käppala area of Lidingö, about ten minutes away. She lived here for the remainder of the ABBA years until she bought her property in Ekerö in the late 80s where she has lived ever since.

Agnetha's home at Jupitervägen from 1978 to the late 1980s.

In late summer of 1979, ABBA did a photo-shoot for the 1979 North American and European tour programme. The pictures depicted each member doing what they enjoyed in their spare time. All of the photos were taken near their homes on Lidingö. Agnetha was pictured with garden shears, Björn while out jogging, Benny by his boat at the local marina and Frida outside "The Pink Villa" with a pile of books. The images chosen for the tour programme were also used for the inside cover of the *Greatest Hits Vol. 2* album.

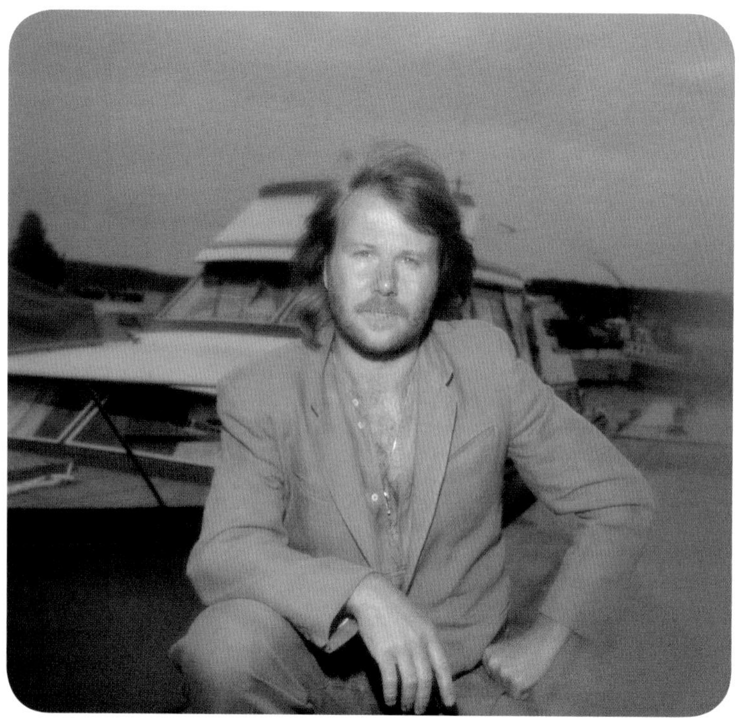

Björn stayed at his and Agnetha's family home. It was here that he posed for pictures with his collie dog Rodde. He stayed there until 1981 when he and his wife Lena moved to Albavägen 7, a traditional yellow-painted house. Björn had married Lena in January 1981.

Frida and Benny stayed at "The Pink Villa" until they split up in early 1981 when both of them moved closer to the city centre. When they moved out, Benny's piano was left behind for the new owners to have.

PLEASE NOTE!
These addresses have had
no connection to ABBA
since 1980s. Please...
respect the current tenants

50

Drottningholms Slott

Drottningholm Palace
Drottningholm

 Brommaplan and then  301-323

www.royalcourt.se

Drottningholms Slott was built in the late 1600s and is today the private home of the Swedish Royal Family who reside in the southern wing, not opened to the public. However, you can enjoy the rest of the palace and the beautiful extensive grounds. There is also the exotic Chinese Pavilion from the 1750s and an 18th century theatre with many of the original features preserved. Drottningholms Slott is on UNESCO's World Heritage list.

In summer 1976, some scenes that were used in four of the five National commercials were filmed at Drottningholms Slott. ABBA were filmed riding bicycles, experimenting with cameras, walkie-talkies and cassette players. Agnetha even put National batteries into a toy donkey!

Filming for the dream sequence in *ABBA – The Movie* took place in June 1977, near Djurgårdskanalen (see p. 108) and Drottningholms Slott. The English Park was the beautiful setting for the picnic and horse-riding scenes.

...Drottningholms Slott

One of the loveliest photo sessions was taken at Drottningholms Slott in summer 1977. Part of the session, where ABBA seemed relaxed and natural, was in front of a row of fountains called "The Cascades" which were built in 1961 following a park restoration. A whole range of photos were taken individually, in pairs and as a group. One of the shots ended up on the single cover of *The Name Of The Game.*

In 1985, when Agnetha had some cover photos taken for her album *Eyes Of A Woman*, one of them was at the balcony at the rear of the palace facing the grounds.

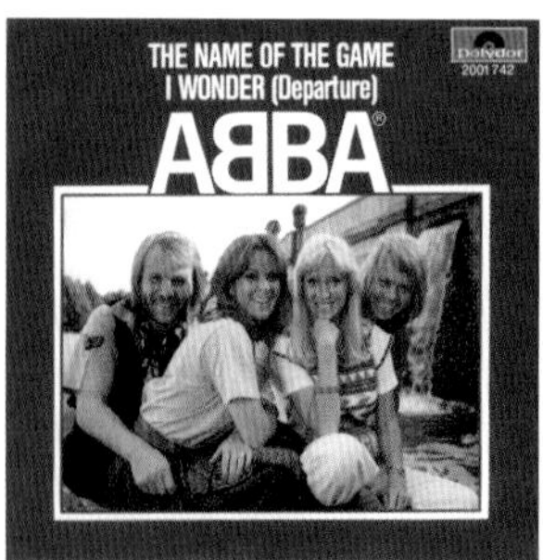

51

Gripsholms Slott

Gripsholm Castle
Mariefred

www.royalcourt.se

Train Stockholm Central to Läggesta, then bus to Mariefred. Or boat from the quay at Stadshuset.

Situated on the edge of lake Mälaren, approximately 70km from Stockholm, Gripsholms Slott is like a fairytale castle keeping watch over the small but pretty and old town of Mariefred. Built by Gustav Vasa in 1537, the castle contains over 400 years of history. You can walk around the castle grounds and see the royal deer at the Hjorthagen nature reserve.

Photographer Ola Lager took ABBA to Gripsholms Slott for the photo session for the *Waterloo* album. He had wanted to take them somewhere historical to fit in with the Waterloo theme.

In the courtyard by the entrance to the castle, ABBA were pictured beating military drums on the cobbled stones.

After you've paid your entrance fee, if you look behind you to the left, you should see steps leading up which look familiar. Here ABBA were photographed sitting in the window area and standing on the steps with "Napoleon", bass player Mike Watson in fact. The picture looking at "Napoleon" was taken on the second floor in room 22, known as *The Audience for the King.*

...Gripsholms Slott

On the third floor of the castle is Gustav III's theatre, an incredibly well-preserved theatre from the 18th century. ABBA were photographed standing on the stage beating military drums for "Napoleon". The theatre was last used in 1987 for the 450th anniversary of the castle in a celebration attended by the Swedish King and Queen.

Also on the third floor, in Room 52, also known as the *Round Room* or *King's Divan Room,* you'll find the set back window where the actual cover picture for *Waterloo* was taken. The paintings on the walls change from time to time but the giveaway is the door to the right of Agnetha.

While on the third floor, check out the *Modern Portrait Gallery,* the oldest portrait collection in the world. The gallery features prominent Swedes from the days of Gustav Vasa up to our very own Benny Andersson! His portrait is by artist Birgit Broms.

NOTE:
YOU ARE NOT ALLOWED TO TAKE PHOTOGRAPHS INSIDE THE CASTLE WITHOUT A SPECIAL PERMIT!...

Europa Film Studios

Tappvägen 24, Bromma

The legendary Europa Film Studios, to the north of Stockholm, was not only of great importance for the Swedish film and television business, it was also one of the leading recording studios from the 50s to the 70s. Due to bad investments, the studios were closed in December 2007 and have since been demolished.

ABBA recorded many of their early music videos at Europa Film Studios, all directed by Lasse Hallström. These included *Ring Ring* and *Waterloo,* filmed on the same day with the same background, as well as *Fernando*.

In the spring of 1979, ABBA filmed two of their music videos for upcoming singles from the *Voulez-Vous* album there: *Does Your Mother Know* and *Voulez-Vous.* The same set was used for both videos, with different stage clothes for each one.

In summer 1979, ABBA made handprints for bronze plaques that were used to decorate Europa Film Studios' new building in Bromma.

For three weeks during August 1979 most of the rehearsals for their forthcoming North American and European Tour took place at Europa Film Studios.

On 3rd October 1980, ABBA filmed the circus crowd scenes for the music video *Super Trouper* at Europa Film Studios. At the same time, the cover photo for the album was taken. The original idea had been for ABBA to be surrounded by circus performers and animals in London's Piccadilly Circus. But they soon discovered that a law was in place prohibiting entertainers and animals from performing on the streets in central London. With Piccadilly Circus in the heart of London's theatre-land, the law was there to discourage theatrical publicity stunts. Plans were changed and Europa Film Studios were hired instead. Party footage used in the music video *Happy New Year* was shot at the same time as *Super Trouper*, only the circus performers were replaced by balloons, streamers and glasses of champagne.

At the time of the filming, the song hadn't been officially named *Super Trouper* so the footage of them actually singing the song was recorded a little while later, also at Europa Film Studios.

In 2003, Benny and Björn won the Swedish Music Publisher's Lifetime Achievement Award for contributions to Swedish music. They were presented with their award by the Swedish Minister of culture at Europa Studios.

NOTE!
Where Europa Film Studios once were located, there is a building site now...
... and nothing to 👁

53

Marcus Studios

Studios 301
Råsundavägen 45, Solna

Pendeltåg from Stockholm Central to Märsta. Get off at Solna.

www.studios301.com

Just like Metronome and Polar Music, Marcus Studios used to be a cinema. Benny's rock group The Hep Stars used it for rehearsals in the 1960s. After changing ownership two to three times since the 1970s, the studios were renamed Studios 301 in 2002. The Swedish rock band Europe recorded their hit *The Final Countdown* here.

In 1977, the year before Polar Music Studios were finished, ABBA recorded most of *ABBA – The Album* at Marcus Studios.

Marcus Studios was chosen over Metronome because recording sessions could be block-booked meaning they were able to spend much longer on their recordings without having to give up the studio for other artists. This was the main reason why they wanted to build their own studio.

During the summer of 1977, Agnetha was pregnant with her son Christian and had to record sessions for *ABBA – The Album* by reclining in a chair to avoid having to stand for long periods. At this time, filming for *ABBA – The Movie* was nearing completion and so ABBA were filmed in Marcus Studios singing *Thank You For The Music*, one of only a handful of songs already recorded for the next album. This performance was seen at the very end of *ABBA – The Movie* and Frida and Agnetha were seen only from the waist up in an attempt to disguise Agnetha's increasingly obvious pregnant state.

Ulriksdals Kyrka

Ulriksdal Church
Slottsallén, Ulriskdal, Solna

 Bergshamra, then  503 to Ulriksdals Wärdshus

Ulriksdals kyrka is close to the Ulriksdals Slott (Ulriksdal Palace) on the banks of Lake Edsviken in the Solna area just north of Stockholm. It was built in the 1860s by architect F W Scholander on behalf of Crown Prince Karl XI and his wife Lovisa.

On 19th May 1980, all ABBA members attended the wedding of Stig's right-hand woman, Görel Johnsen to photographer Anders Hanser at Ulriksdal kyrka. Agnetha attended with her new boyfriend Dick Håkansson who she had only been dating a few weeks.

Vallentuna

Agnetha & Björn, Rosengårdsvägen 87
Frida & Benny, Rosengårdsvägen 115

Take the train Roslagsbanan from Stockholms Östra towards Kårsta and get off at Vallentuna station.

In early 1972, both couples moved to Vallentuna, a suburb about an hour to the north of Stockholm.

They both moved into very similar single-level houses in a dense area called Rosendal. The houses, which looked fairly basic for well-known pop stars, were situated less than 100m apart from each other on Rosengårdsvägen, with Agnetha and Björn living at No. 87 and Frida and Benny living at No. 115. Here they spent a lot of time together writing, singing, playing music and socialising.

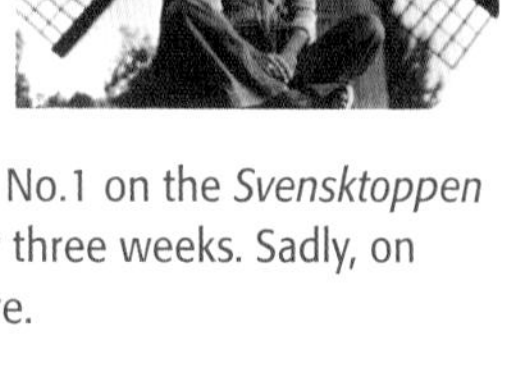

During the summer of 1972, Benny and Frida were photographed in front of a windmill in Vallentuna which was within 350m of their house. One of the photos was subsequently used as the cover picture for Frida's solo single *Man vill ju leva lite dessemellan* (You've got to live a little every now and then). The single went to No.1 on the *Svensktoppen* (Swedish Top Ten) radio charts and stayed there for three weeks. Sadly, on 29th March 2008, the windmill was destroyed by fire.

Frida & Benny's house.

Agnetha & Björn's house.

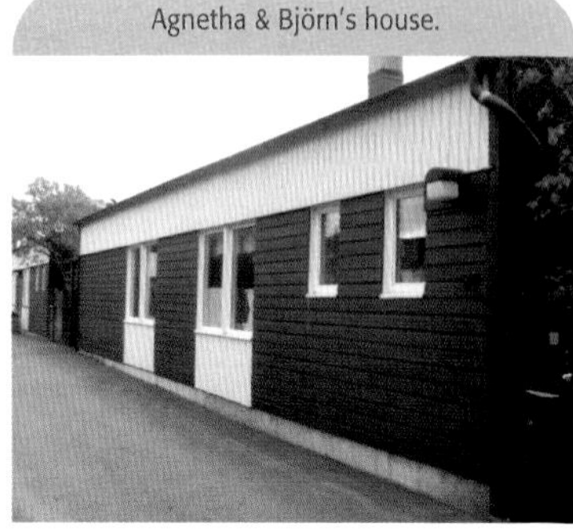

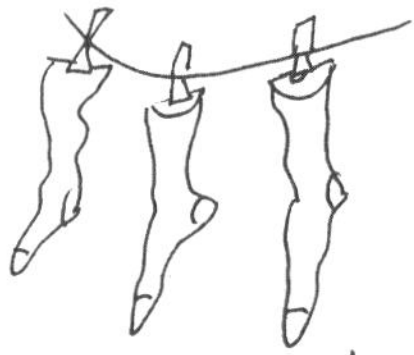

These [houses] Houses
No Longer have
anything to do
with ABBA.
PLEAAASE... respect
the privacy of the
current OWNERS.

Nr 43 17. Okt 1974 C 1917 CX
BRAVO
Mit Foto-Love Story!!!
SERIE:
ABBA INTIM
2 GLÜCKLICHE PAARE
Ganz groß in Farbe: Maggie Mae und Keith Emerson
SWEET!
auf Deutschland-Tournee
BRAVO-Reporterin bei einem Jungen im Gefängnis

In 1974, photographer "Bubi" Heilemann did a couple of extensive photo-shoots in Vallentuna for BRAVO magazine. The most memorable was taken behind Agnetha and Björn's home with ABBA posing on a rock.

Barkarby Airport

Järfälla

Pendeltåg Barkarby

The Barkarby airport used to be a Swedish Air Force base to the north-west of Stockholm in an area called Järfälla. For many years it was one of Sweden's longest serving airports and had its own local flying club. The last commercial flight was in December 2008.

Barkarby was the location used to photograph the 1976 cover of the *Arrival* album. ABBA also posed standing in front of the helicopter on the airfield. This picture was used on the inside LP sleeve.

The idea for holding the photo-shoot at the airfield was a joint one between designer Rune Söderqvist and photographer Ola Lager. The photographs were taken late in the early evening, during sunset. As Ola explained, *"There was no Photoshop in those days!"*, meaning the pictures have not been manipulated digitally with a computer.

Ola Lager had some difficulties communicating with the pilot to get the helicopter at the right angle and so it had to take off and land several times. On one of those occasions Benny went up in the helicopter with Ola's two daughters.

Barkarby can be reached by the local train "pendeltåg" from Stockholm Central, heading to Bålsta or Jakobsberg. It is only four stops (about 14 min) from Stockholm Central. However, there is nothing to see now. You might be interested to know that there is an IKEA superstore located nearby.

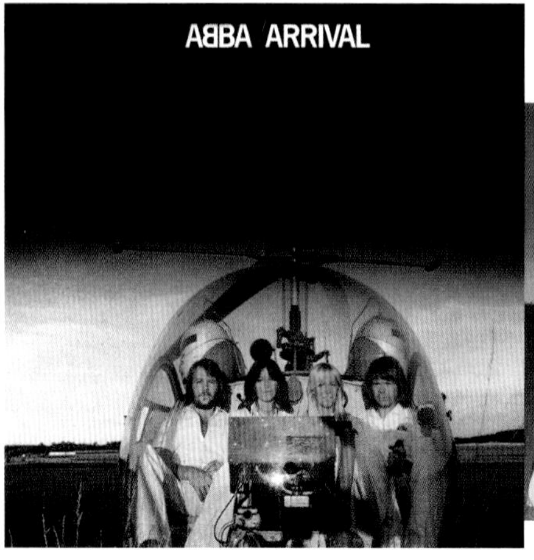

ABBA

57

Glen Studio

Vallvägen 2, Stocksund

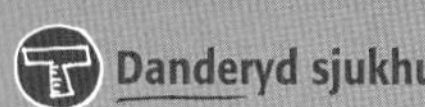

Danderyd sjukhus

With studio time becoming scarce at the popular Metronome Studios (see p. 28), some of ABBA's early recordings, including *So Long, Hey Hey Helen, Man In The Middle* and *SOS* were laid down at Glen Studio, part of Bruno Glenmark's home. Agnetha also recorded some of her 1975 solo album *Elva kvinnor i ett hus* here.

Benny, Björn and ABBA-guitarist Janne Schaffer used the swimming pool area in the house as an echo chamber.

IMPORTANT

Please note that this is no longer a studio OR associated with ABBA in any way. Please respect the privacy of the current owners.

ABBA on swings in the back garden

Viggsö

Stockholm archipelago

Viggsö is one of 30,000 islands in the Stockholm archipelago, a beautiful maze of pine-covered islands stretching 80km to the east of Stockholm city. Some are dotted with wooden houses while others are entirely deserted. There are unspoilt beaches and plenty of rocks and wildlife. Viggsö is approximately the same size as Gamla Stan and is on the main shipping route from Stockholm to Riga. Many of the islands in the archipelago can be reached by boat from central Stockholm departing from Strömkajen and Strandvägen. Viggsö is not one of them – the nearest island is its much larger neighbour, Grinda.

Agnetha and Björn bought a summer house on Viggsö in 1972. Frida and Benny bought theirs in autumn 1973. Manager Stig Anderson had owned a house there for a number of years before the ABBA members joined him.

Having a summer house is a long tradition in Sweden. Every year thousands of Swedes migrate to the countryside for some rest and relaxation during the summer months. At the foot of Agnetha and Björn's property on Viggsö was a small cabin with very basic facilities overlooking the water. There was just enough room for a piano and a couple of chairs. Here Benny and Björn would "jam" together, playing piano and guitar, until a new tune appeared. Most of ABBA's early music started life on Viggsö including *Fernando* and *Dancing Queen.*

Björn explained to Australian TV host Don Lane in 1977 that the island had about 40 summer houses on it. Many early press reports gave the impression that ABBA owned the actual island but over time it became apparent that they just owned a couple of private houses on the island, which was pretty exclusive as public boat trips did not – and still don't – stop there.

Benny explained at the time, *"When we're not working, we all enjoy doing nothing. We go to our holiday island outside Stockholm to soak up the sun. Out there you can really get stuck into things. No unwanted phone calls, no recording studios, nothing. We just write and eat and down the odd beer or something a bit stronger."*

Frida added, *"When I go out on the island, all the stress disappears and I can get back to normal. I can be at peace with myself. The island is very well located. People almost never go ashore there."*

Björn commented, *"It is marvelous there. The girls can drag their feet and we can go for wonderful voyages in our motorboat. The days on our island are very relaxing ones for us. They are a respite from our heavy work schedule."*

In 1976, one of the first film crews to travel to Viggsö and film ABBA's secret hideaway, was the team for the programme *ABBA-dabba-dooo!!* Here they were interviewed; Benny and Björn were seen jamming in their cabin and Frida walked around the shores of the island for a performance of *Knowing Me, Knowing You*. This was the programme where they were seen laughing like drains!

In 1977 the film crew for *ABBA – The Movie* spent a weekend on Viggsö while they filmed the "pullout" shot of the island from the helicopter. Actor Robert Hughes, who played Ashley in the film, was hiding behind Benny and Björn's cabin as the helicopter pulled away.

Many photo sessions took place on Viggsö in the early ABBA years although these seemed to stop after the 1977 filming for *ABBA – The Movie.*

In 1999, Björn revisited the cabin for *The Winner Takes It All – The ABBA Story* and recalled how he and Benny worked there all those years previously. He had done the same for a Swedish travel programme a few years earlier as well.

In 2005, Björn bought a house on Viggsö from Lasse Anderson, the son of Stig. His wife Lena told the press, *"Now that we have two summer cabins the whole family can come out if they want to. We like to spend time in the archipelago. It is so relaxing with the silence. And it's going to be nice to sit there and read and do our crosswords when we get older."*

...Appendix for super fans

Note: These destinations are not marked on the map.

Berns is a hotel, nightclub and restaurant complex where ABBA filmed the *Hovas Vittne* video. Located next door to China Teatern.
T-bana Kungsträdgården

Kungsträdgården is a large tree-lined leisure area around the corner from the old Polar Music offices (Hamngatan). It was here where Agnetha skated in *A For Agnetha* and where Frida was interviewed for the US programme *Freeze Frame,* outside the restaurant *T.G.I. Friday's* with fountains in the background.
T-bana Kungsträdgården

Tornbergs ur is the clock tower that appears at the end of *ABBA – The Movie.* The clock with its significant, green pointed top can be found opposite Dramaten, at Nybroplan/Berzelii Park. T-bana Kungsträdgården

Strömparterren is where Frida was filmed singing *Saltwater*, leaning against some railings, and was also interviewed for the Swedish programme *Sommarfolk* in 1992. Strömparterren is situated under Norrbro, the bridge linking Kungliga Operan and Kungliga Slottet. T-bana Kungsträdgården

Summer Night City video – the scene with Frida and Benny walking down the street next to a traffic barrier was shot in Stallgatan at the Nybroviken bay.
T-bana Kungsträdgården

Strandvägen is a long stretch of grand houses and a tree-lined road all the way along the water's edge from Nybroplan to Djurgårdsbron. Here ABBA walked in *ABBA in Sweden* with Ian "Molly" Meldrum in 1976. Two years later Agnetha and Björn were seen strolling together at dusk in a scene in the music video *Summer Night City.* Also, Frida and Benny were pictured here with Nordiska Museet in the background. T-bana Kungsträdgården

A For Agnetha – Peder Fredags gränd is the alleyway where Agnetha hid from the children in the program *A For Agnetha.* (Note, today there is a gate preventing you from entering.) Chased by the children, Agnetha also runs from the archway Stora Hoparegränd into Österlånggatan towards the St. George statue, and then right up into Bollhusgränd. T-bana Gamla Stan

Birger Jarls Torg is a public square on Riddarholmen where some parts of Agnetha's 1987 music video *I Wasn't The One (Who Said Goodbye)* was filmed. You could see her leaning against the wall of Stenbockska Palatset, and cycling past the building. At the opposite end of the square are the railings that Agnetha stood in front of in the video. T-bana Gamla Stan

Lasse Hallström's apartment – here, the music videos to both *One Of Us* and *Happy New Year* were filmed. The apartment is at Karlavägen 83, parallel to Strandvägen. Today, the apartment is a private address with no ABBA connection. Please do not disturb the occupants. T-bana Karlaplan

Berwaldhallen is a concert hall where *Chess In Concert* was performed in 1984. Frida joined the choir for the recording of the titletrack of Benny's 1987 Album *Klinga Mina Klockor* here. She also attended several Polar Music Prize ceremonies here in the late 90s and early 00s. T-bana Karlaplan

Bang A Boomerang – the music video was filmed on southern Djurgården in April 1975. The two main areas of filming were right by the water's edge on a narrow path where the land juts out (opposite Manillaskolan, where Manillavägen and Djurgårdsvägen cross) and by some trees a few feet from the shore. Bus 69 Manillavägen

Årstabron is the bridge that can be seen in ABBA's music video *The Day Before You Came*. Today there is a new bridge alongside the old one, and there is no direct view of Årstabron. However you can get a glimpse of it from Liljeholmsbron, the nearest bridge. T-bana Hornstull

Tumba Station is the train station which was featured in the music video *The Day Before You Came*, where Agnetha was waiting on the platform. Take the "pendeltåg" from Stockholm Central, heading towards Gnesta or Södertälje Centralen.

This book presents most of the main ABBA-related places in Stockholm but some of the ABBA story took place in other cities and towns in Sweden. Here are some of the most important.

Eskilstuna

From the age of two, Frida grew up with her grandmother in Torshälla, just outside Eskilstuna. As a young adult she lived here with her husband and children, before moving to Stockholm in 1969.

Göteborg

- Björn was born here on 25th April 1945.
- Agnetha, Benny, Björn and Anni-Frid's first stage performance together was at Trägår'n on 1st November 1970. Note, the current building at Nya Allén 11 is not the same as the one in 1970.
- ABBA's first Folkpark tour started on 15th June 1973 at Liseberg's Amusement Park. You can find ABBA's handprints and a star on the ground near the entrance.
- At Bohus Studios in Kungsbacka, ABBA mixed *The Name Of The Game* and worked on the soundtrack for *ABBA – The Movie* in 1977.
- At Scandinavium, Agnetha starred in *Jesus Christ Superstar* premièring on 18th February 1972. Here ABBA also performed live in January 1975, January 1977 and October 1979.

Hova
Stig Anderson was born here. Today there is a bronze bust in his honour.

Jönköping
Agnetha was born here on 5th April 1950. This is also where she grew up.

Linköping
Benny and Björn met here for the first time at a party for the Hootenanny Singers who had been called up for military service.

Malmö
Benny and Björn's musical *Kristina från Duvemåla* premièred at the Malmö Music Theatre on 7th October 1995, attended by Agnetha.

Marstrand
The Winner Takes It All music video was filmed here, just north of Göteborg. The inside shots were filmed at the Societetshuset (Society house).

Västervik
Björn grew up here from the age of six after moving from Göteborg.

Verum
Agnetha and Björn got married here in July 1971 at Verum church, north of Hässleholm.

...Recommended books and websites

Recommended books & publications

From ABBA To Mamma Mia! by Anders Hanser & Carl Magnus Palm (2010)
ABBA In America by Leif Schulman & Charles Hammarsten (2010)
Benny's Road To ABBA by Carl Magnus Palm (2004)
ABBA – Photographs 1974-1980 by Wolfgang Heilemann (2004)
Bright Lights, Dark Shadows by Carl Magnus Palm (2001)
ABBA – The Book by Jean-Marie Potiez (2000)
ABBA – The Complete Recording Sessions by Carl Magnus Palm (1994)
ABBA Intermezzo the international fan club magazine (since 1990)
The Official International Fan Club Magazine (since 1986)
ABBA In Their Own Words compiled by Rosemary York (1981)
ABBA The Ultimate Pop Group by Marianne Lindvall (1977)
The ABBA Phenomenon (ABBA by ABBA) as told to Christer Borg (1977)
The Official ABBA Magazine (1977–1983)

Websites

www.abbafanclub.nl
The Official ABBA Fan Club, based in the Netherlands.

www.abba4ever.com
ABBA fan community.

www.abba4therecord.com
Collection of ABBA LPs & CDs from all around the world.

www.abba-intermezzo.de
Intermezzo, the international ABBA Fan Club and magazine, started in 1990.

www.abbaworld.com
Infosite about the official ABBA-endorsed exhibition, and the world's largest ABBA merchandise shop.

www.icethesite.com
Devoted to news about Benny & Björn and their music projects, with emphasis on the musicals *Chess* and *Kristina från Duvemåla*.

http://abbaarticles.blogspot.com
ABBA articles from the Netherlands, Belgium and Germany translated into English.

http://home.zipworld.com.au/~callisto/abba.html
The Worldwide ABBA Chart Lists.

Acknowledgements

ABBAMAIL, ABBA Report, ABBA Village, Mats Andersson, Micke Andersson, Robin Andersson, Heinz Angermayr, Frank Axelsson, Neil Barber, Marcus Benson, Inez Buijtenhek, Chris Childs, Ian Cole, Matti Crocker, Cliff Docherty, Essential Stockholm, David Fyfe, Regina Grafunder, Anders Hanser, Alex-Zsolt Hegedüs, Micke Hjernestam, Frank Horstmann, Ian Jones, Rod Kirkman, Ola Lager, Bengt H. Malmqvist, Wolfgang "Bubi" Heilemann, Sarah McSharry, Claudia Menzi, Jörgen Parys, Pepé, Raffe Pohlman, Daphne Simonds, Michael Teske, Gareth Thomas, Robert Verbeek, Amanda Walters

A special thanks to Carl Magnus Palm for fact-checking and additional research.

Thanks to Paul & Joey Jack Russell and my parents for all their love and support.

Photo credits

Billy Adolfsson 12 right, 17b, 17 left, 20b, 30, 31b, 42b, 43, 44, 46, 53b, 55, 56b, 57-58, 60b, 68-69; Mats Andersson 24, 26b, 30b; Michael Brannäs / Scanpix 91; Claudio Bresciani / Scanpix 41 left; Torbjörn Calvero / Premium Rockshot, 128b, 129 above, 146b, 147b; Mattias Carlsson / Aftonbladet Bild 92 below; Liska Cersowsky / Premium Rockshot 10b, 22b, 25b, 28b, 34b, 52b, 62b, 64b, 67, 71b, 71 left, 72b, 78b, 82b, 82-83, 86b, 88b, 94b, 97 below, 98 below, 99, 100b, 106b, 107, 108b, 110 below, 112b, 113 above, 114b; Alexis Daflos / Kungl. Hovstaterna 122b, 125b; Hans T Dahlskog / Scanpix 51; Cliff Docherty 19b, 40b, 48b, 54b, 59b, 90b; Getty Images / Redfern Collection 84; Jonny Graan / Scanpix 140; Regina Grafunder 117 below, 120 below; Björn Gullander / Scanpix 16; Charles Hammarsten 12 (IBL Bildbyrå), 17 above (IBL Bildbyrå), 49 above, 114 above, 128, 134 left; Anders Hanser / Premium Rockshot 17 right, 18, 20-21, 32b, 33, 34, 36-38, 49 below, 50, 75, 76-77, 104b, 104-105, 112 below, 114 below, 121, 129 below, 130-131, 144 below, 147b, 148-149; Alex-Zsolt Hegedüs 47b, 66b, 70b, 80b, 110 above right, 146b; Wolfgang Bubi Heilemann 53, 59, 62-63, 66, 115; Janerik Henriksson / Scanpix 113 below; Fredrik Hessman / IBL Bildbyrå 45 below; Ulf Holmstedt / Scanpix 42; Anders Jahrner / IBL Bildbyrå 14 above; Peter Kjellerås / Aftonbladet Bild 15; Ola Lager / Premium Rockshot 7, 27, 48, 102, 118-120 above, 126-127, 139; Lars Larsson / Premium Rockshot 95; Barry Levine 123 below; Bengt H Malmqvist / Premium Rockshot 6, 10-11, 23 above, 25, 33 above, 35, 40, 61, 72, 73-74, 79-81, 85-89, 100-101, 108-109, 116, 123 above, 124 above, 132, 133 below, 134 right & below, 141-144 above, 145, 142 above, 143; Saxon & Lindströms / IBL Bildbyrå 90; Sarah McSharry 136; Nils Petter Nilsson / Scanpix 41 right; Stefan Nilsson / Aftonbladet Bild 52; Pressens Bild / Scanpix 13; Sara Russell 12b, 13b, 15b, 16b, 84b, 96 below, 117 above, 124 below, 125, 134b, nner flap back cover; Sanna Sjöswärd / Aftonbladet Bild 65; Sjöberg Bild 135, 136-137; Sven-Erik Sjöberg / Scanpix 64; Mats Strand / Aftonbladet Bild 29; Svenskt Pressfoto / Scanpix 133 above; Karin Törnblom / IBL Bildbyrå 23 below, 45 above, 92 above, 93, 98 above; Amanda Walters 136; Wille Wendt / Premium Rockshot 132b, 135b, 138b, 140b; Cover and inner flap front cover: all pictures Premium Rockshot

Banner pictures are indicated with the letter "b" after the page number (e.g. 17b).

Every effort has been made to acknowledge correctly and contact the source and/or copywright holder of each illustration. We apologise for any unintentional errors or omissions.

THE PREMIUM COLLECTION...

The EP Book
– Swedish Rock & Pop Pressings
1954–1969
by Roger Holegård
SOLD OUT

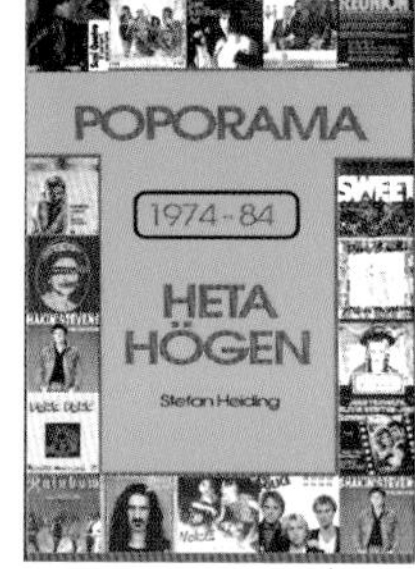

Poporama
– Heta Högen 1974–1984
by Stefan Heiding
SOLD OUT

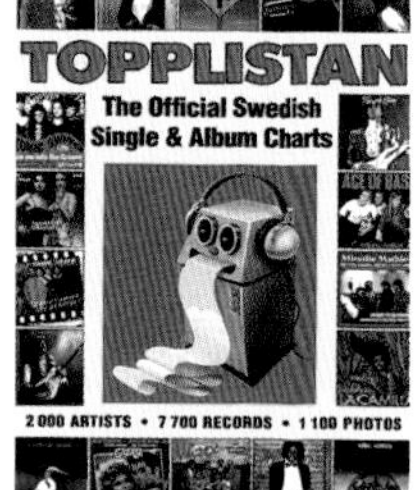

Topplistan
– The Official Swedish Single &
Album Charts 1975–1993
by Wille Wendt
SOLD OUT

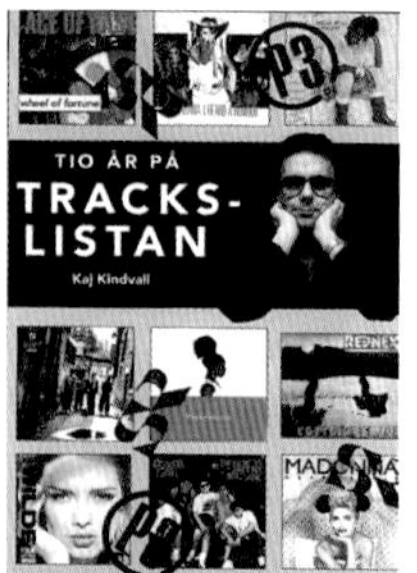

Tio år på Trackslistan
by Kaj Kindvall
SOLD OUT

Stora Popboken
– Svensk Rock & Pop 1954–1969
by Hans Olofsson
Discopraphies: Sture Hallberg
SOLD OUT

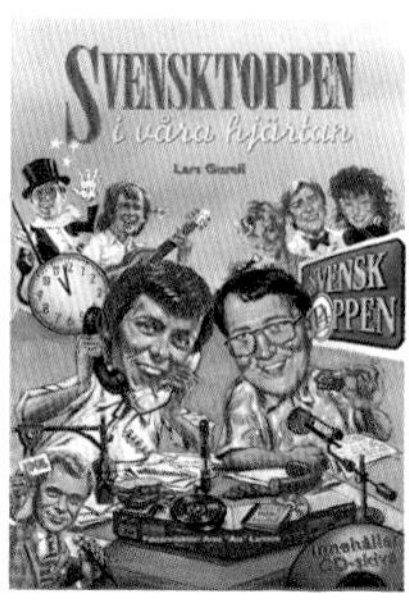

Svensktoppen i våra hjärtan
by Lars Gurell
Bonus CD included
SOLD OUT

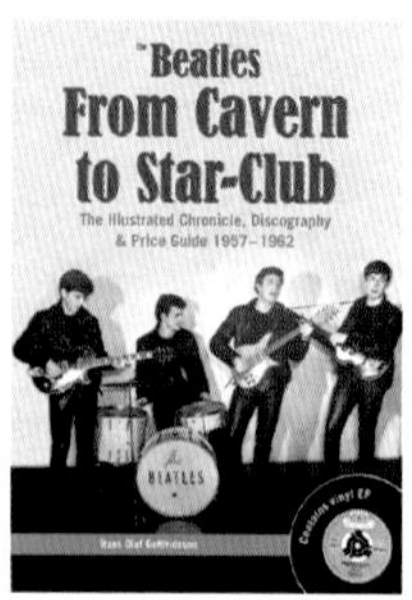

The Beatles
– From Cavern to Star-Club
by Hans Olof Gottfridsson
Bonus vinyl EP included

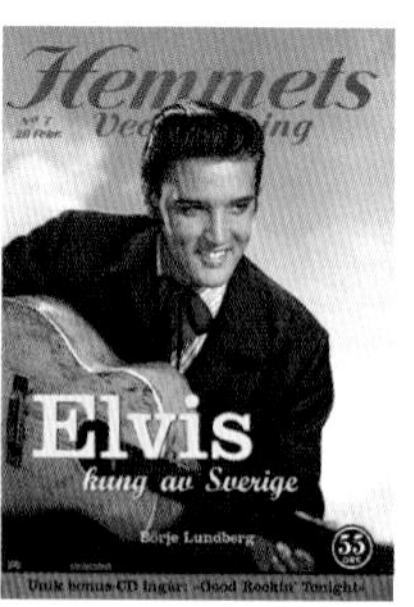

Elvis – Kung av Sverige
by Börje Lundberg
Bonus CD included
Also in paperback without CD
SOLD OUT

Lyckliga Gatan
– du finns inte mer...
by Britt Lindeborg
SOLD OUT

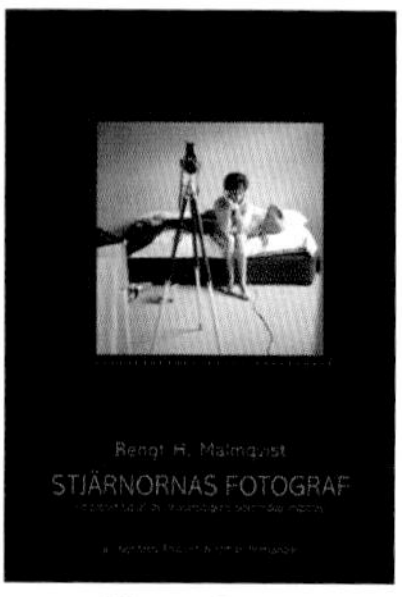

Stjärnornas Fotograf
– Bengt H. Malmqvist
by Kenneth Ahlborn & Urban Nilmander
8 postcards included
SOLD OUT

The Rolling Stones i Sverige
– från Baltiska Hallen till Bredäng
by Börje Lundberg & Ove Tingvall
Bonus CD included

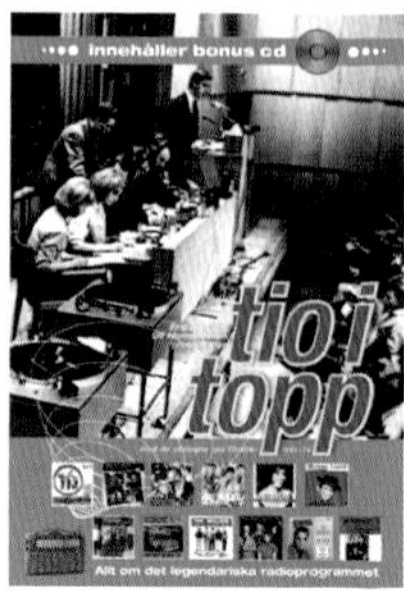

Tio i Topp – med de utslagna
på försök 1961–74
by Eric Hallberg & Ulf Henningsson
Bonus CD included

Från ABBA till Mamma Mia!
by Carl Magnus Palm
& Anders Hanser

Visa oss vinden
– Bob Dylan i Sverige
by Göran Holmquist
Bonus CD included
SOLD OUT

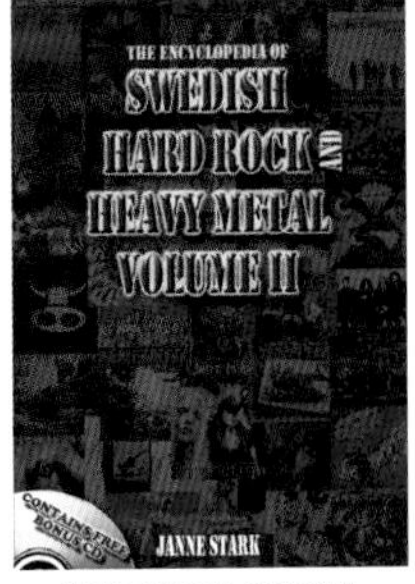

The Encyclopedia of Swedish Hard Rock and Heavy Metal Vol II
by Janne Stark
Bonus CD included

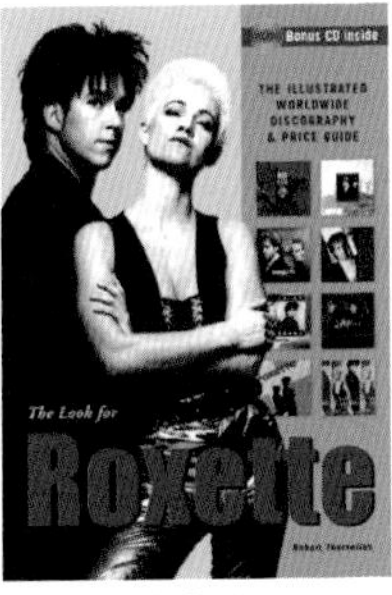

The Look for Roxette – The Illustrated Worldwide Discography & Price Guide
by Robert Thorselius
Bonus CD included

Tio liv
by Ludde Lindström

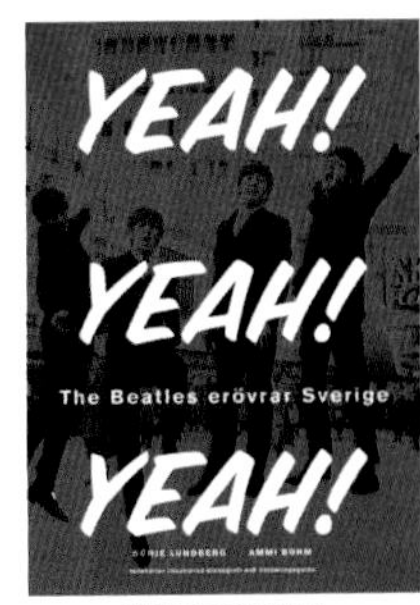

YEAH! YEAH! YEAH! – The Beatles erövrar Sverige
by Börje Lundberg & Ammi Bohm
Bonus CD included

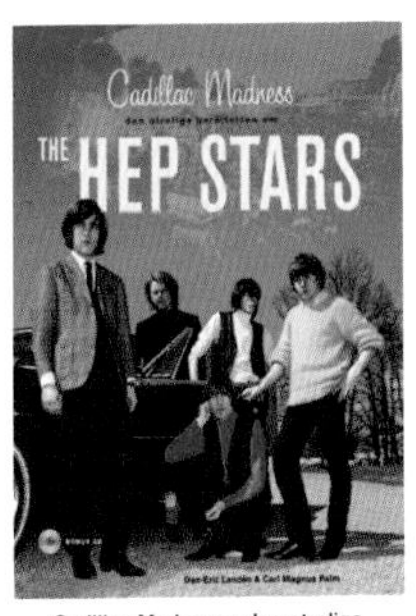

Cadillac Madness – den otroliga berättelsen om The Hep Stars
by Dan-Eric Landén
& Carl Magnus Palm
Bonus CD included

Benny's Road to ABBA
by Carl Magnus Palm

Opera!
– De 30 bästa genom tiderna
by Mats Bäcker, Ditte Feuk
& Jan Larsson

Eurovision Song Contest 50 år – Den officiella jubileumsboken
by John Kennedy O'Connor

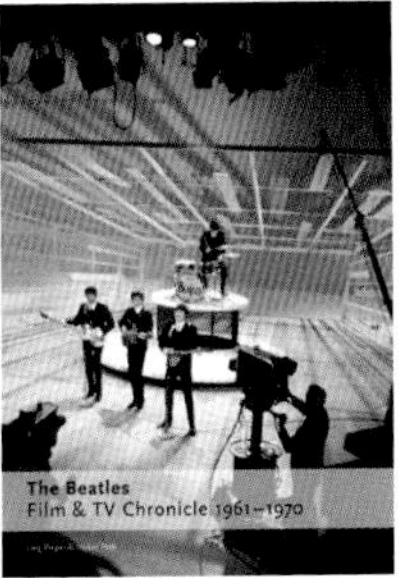

The Beatles – Film & TV Chronicle 1961–1970
by Jörg Pieper & Volker Path

Stora Schlagerboken – De svenska sångerskorna 1954–1969 Volym I/A–L
by Hans Olofsson & Leif Aulin

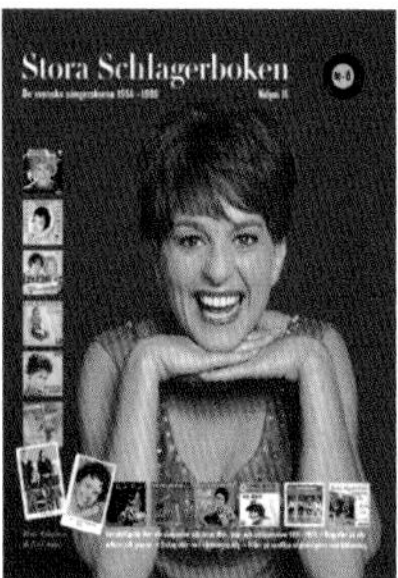

Stora Schlagerboken
– De svenska sångerskorna 1954–1969
Volym II/M–Ö
by Hans Olofsson & Leif Aulin

Stora Schlagerboxen
– 100 svenska sångerskor 1954–1969
4 CD-box with 48-page booklet
Liner notes by Hans Olofsson
SOLD OUT

Melodifestivalen genom tiderna
– De svenska uttagningarna och internationella finalerna
by Leif Thorsson & Martin Verhage

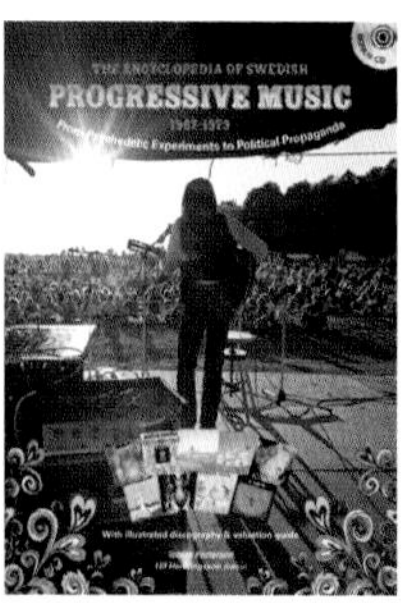

The Encyclopedia of Swedish Progressive Music 1967–1979
by Tobias Petterson & Ulf Henningsson (editor)
Bonus CD included
SOLD OUT

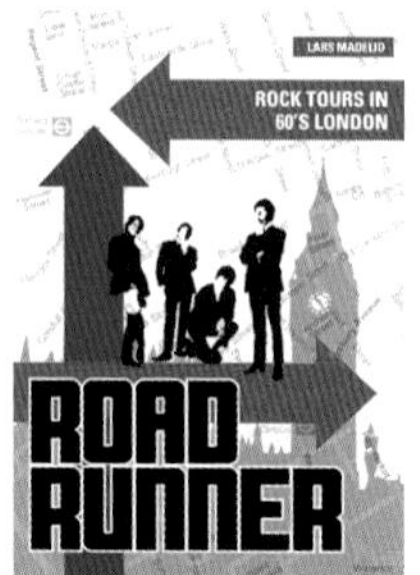

Roadrunner
– Rock Tours In 60's London
by Lars Madelid
English version
Swedish version available

John Lennon var min bror, jag svär!
by Bengt Nyman

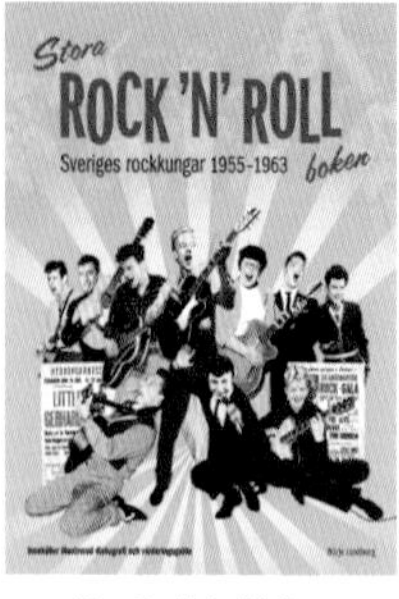

Stora Rock 'n' roll-boken
– Sveriges rockkungar 1955–1963
by Börje Lundberg
Bonus poster included

The Essence of Swedish Progressive Music 1967–1979
4 CD-box with 48-page booklet
Liner notes by Ulf Henningsson
SOLD OUT

Stora Rock 'n' roll-boxen
– Svensk rock 'n' roll 1954–1963
4 CD-box with 48-page booklet
Liner notes by Börje Lundberg
SOLD OUT

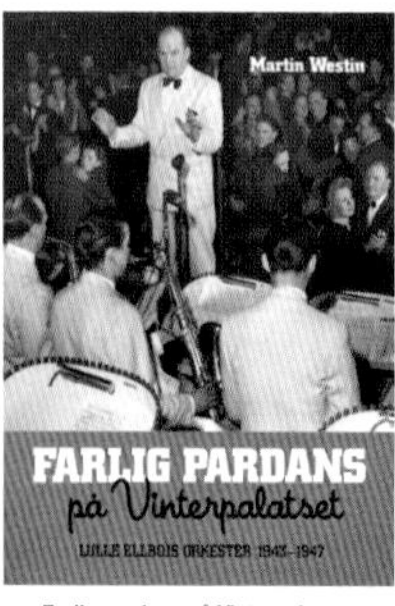

Farlig pardans på Vinterpalatset
– Lulle Ellbojs orkester 1943–1947
by Martin Westin

The Encyclopedia of Swedish Punk 1977–1987
by Peter Jandréus

Stora Schlagerboxen
– 100 svenska sångerskor 1954-1969
4 CD-box with 48-page booklet
Liner notes by Hans Olofsson

Poster
– Nordens största Poptidning 1974-1980
by Fabian H. Bernstone & Mathias Brink
Bonus poster included

Labelography
– The Major U.K. Record Labels
by Jan Pettersson

Radiogrammofonen
– en harmoni i klang och elegans
by Lars-Göran Dybeck

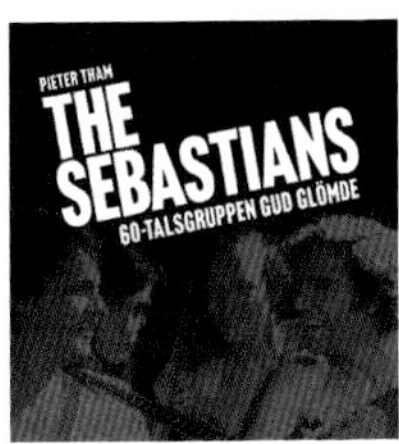

The Sebastians
– 60-talsgruppen Gud glömde
by Pieter Tham
Bonus CD included

The EP Book – Swedish Rock & Pop Pressings 1954-1969
Second edition
by Roger Holegård & Ulf Henningsson

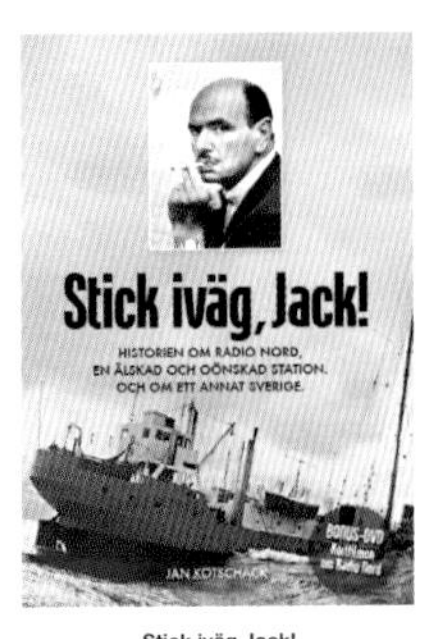

Stick iväg Jack!
– Historien om Radio Nord
by Jan Kotschack
Bonus DVD included

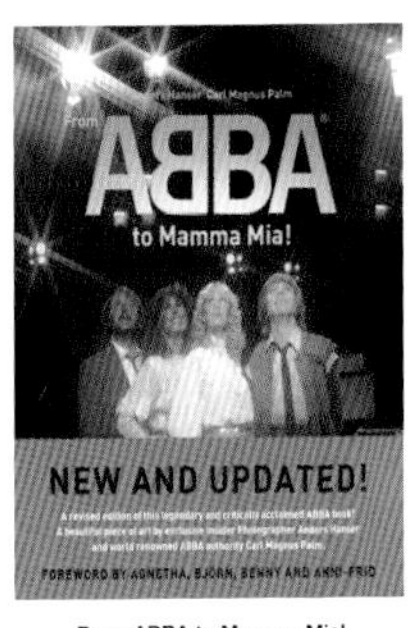

From ABBA to Mamma Mia!
New & Updated
by Carl Magnus Palm & Anders Hanser
English edition

De legendariska åren
– Metronome Records
by Håkan Lahger & Lasse Ermalm
Edition with bonus CD SOLD OUT
Second edition in new size

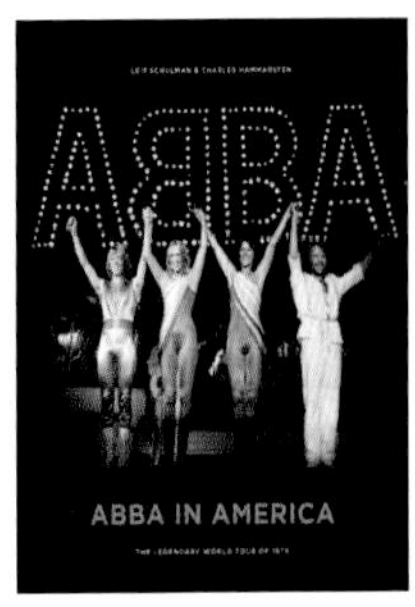

ABBA in America
by Charles Hammarsten & Leif Schulman
English edition

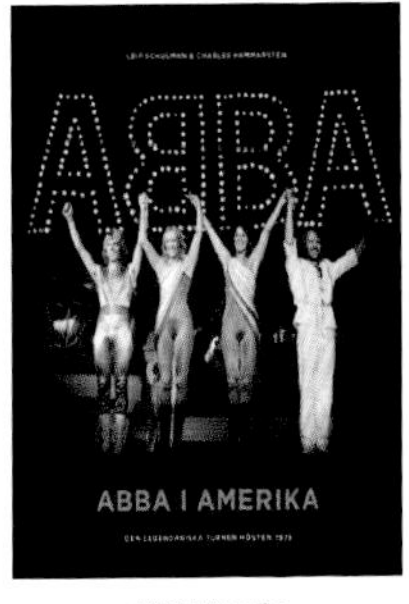

ABBA i Amerika
by Charles Hammarsten & Leif Schulman
Swedish edition

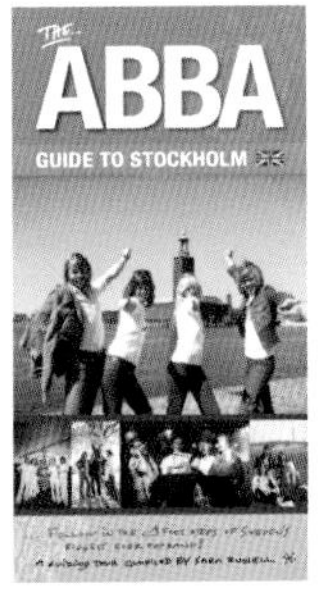

The ABBA Guide to Stockholm
by Sara Russell
English edition

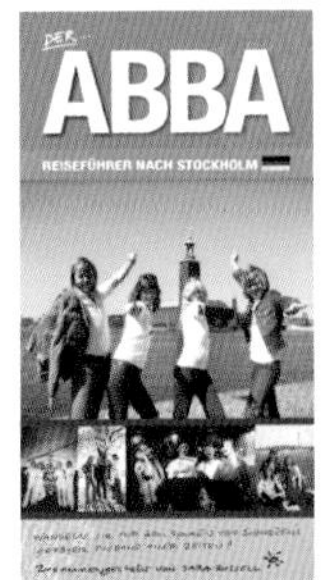

Der ABBA Reiseführer nach Stockholm
by Sara Russell
German edition

Hejdå... Come Back Soon!